For a Meaningful Life (No Matter What's Happened)

PAM CORDANO, MFT

To Viktor Frankl, with Love

BALBOA.PRESS
A DIVISION OF HAY HOUSE

Balboa Press books may be ordered through booksellers or by contacting:

Balboa Press
A Division of Hay House
1663 Liberty Drive
Bloomington, IN 47403
www.balboapress.com
1 (877) 407-4847

Print information available on the last page.

ISBN: 978-1-9822-4134-6 (sc)
ISBN: 978-1-9822-4136-0 (hc)
ISBN: 978-1-9822-4135-3 (e)

Library of Congress Control Number: 2020900646

Balboa Press rev. date: 01/14/2020

Contents

Introduction

It wasn't until I was 46 years old that I was sure I wanted to be alive.

Before that I lived on a fence, with life on one side and death on the other. I couldn't climb down off the fence to fully embrace my life because I didn't know how. But I also couldn't justify leaving my kids without their mom. So I waited in limbo.

Over my 27-year career as a therapist I have worked with people living on a similar fence, also in limbo. Maybe they have a deadly disease and ask, *How much more suffering can I take?* Maybe they've lost their child or their beloved and ask, *What's the point of being alive without them?* Maybe they are disabled and wonder, *Why should I even be here when I can't do the most basic things for myself?*

Others can't point to a specific tragedy but feel a chronic deadness inside. While merely going through the motions of life, they say, *Nothing inspires me anymore. I don't feel a sense of purpose.*

If you know this fence, if you know that limbo, this book is for you.

These 10 Foundations are the very essence of what helped me to finally get off the fence and choose life. I hope they help you choose life, too.

In this book I want to single out what helps and what doesn't. I want to save you time, money that you might spend on years of therapy, and unnecessary pain on your path to a wholehearted life.

In practical and efficient ways, I have distilled the most powerful lessons I've learned to help you create a gorgeous life on your terms—no matter what's happened.

Coming fully alive is your birthright.

Dedication

My muse is Viktor Frankl, Holocaust survivor. I talk about him a lot. I needed to learn from someone who knew hate and humiliation and the end of a world. I needed a real-life person who'd come back from all that, who believed in life more than death, and who fell in love with his future, despite his tragic past.

In fact, Viktor Frankl decided that some of the most horrific cruelty and pain he experienced in the death camps of the Holocaust would be his biggest teachers. I needed that kind of perspective and courage to help me get off the damn fence. He was big and bold enough to reach me, not only in the horrors he suffered but in how he raised the bar for all of us to say Yes to life despite any circumstances we've suffered. *Any circumstances,* with no exceptions.

> *I dedicate this book to you, Viktor. Your valiant efforts in the midst of unimaginable suffering translated through religions, cultures, languages, and eras, providing a bridge to life that I could walk across. You helped me choose to leave an internal frozenness and risk moving toward a full expression of my human spirit. You offered a map from despair to joy. You showed me why I should understand that life itself is asking something of me, and the only thing that makes any sense, despite it all, is to uncurl my hand and reach out, finally, to take hold of life's hand and say a wholehearted Yes.*

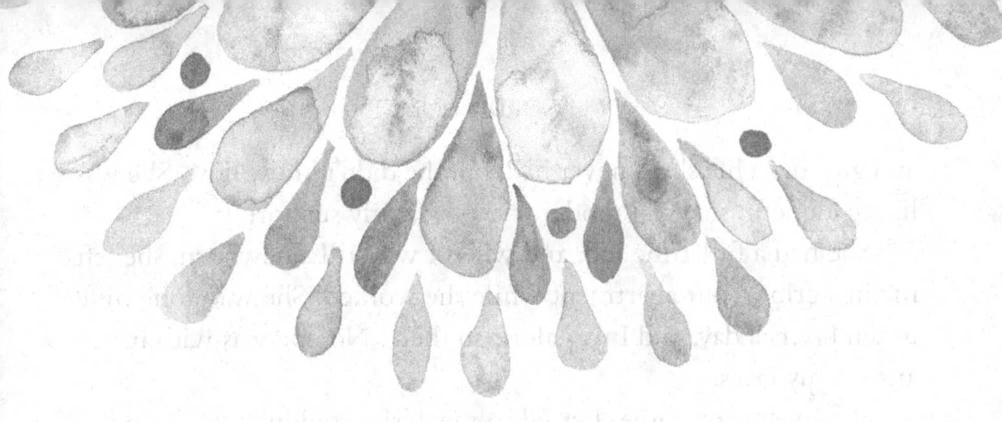

Chapter 1

BONDING (VS. LONELINESS)

There's a way out of loneliness, and it's called bonding. I didn't know this, and it wasn't until I was almost 50 years old that my therapist taught me what bonding actually is.

He said, "Bonding = Call + Response."

A Call is an ask for help. When we ask someone for help, directly or indirectly, and they Respond kindly to us enough times, we begin to trust them. We start to feel a bond with them. That's how it works.

It begins when we're babies. We Call to our moms with our cries. We're hungry, tired, bored, or uncomfortable, and hopefully she Responds with feeding us, helping us get to sleep, playing with us, or holding us.

Bonding is at the very basis of human survival and connection. We all need it to live. People who don't get enough of it suffer and die.

Bonding is a very big deal.

When I was born in 1965, my mom was 18 and mentally ill. She'd been raised and abused in orphanages since she was two, so she didn't know much about bonding either. She wanted to keep me and give me a life she'd never had, but she didn't know how. She was living alone in survival mode, without family support.

She had a full-time job, and when I was still a newborn, she left me in a crib in our apartment while she worked. She was gone nine to ten hours a day, and I was alone in there. No one was with me to answer my cries.

When she got home, I cried so much she couldn't take it, so she hit me and shook me to make me stop.

She was seeing a psychiatrist at the county hospital and told him what was going on. He knew I was in danger (he heard my Call for help through her story), and he worked with the police to get me out of there. I went to a foster home for a month. He maintained a good relationship with my mom in the process, which is amazing because once you have a mom's baby taken away from her, maintaining her trust is nearly impossible.

After a month in that foster home, I was returned to my mom, and it happened all over again. She left me alone while she worked, and when she got home and I cried, she hit me and shook me. She told the psychiatrist, and again he called the police, and they removed me. I was placed in a second foster home. He kept seeing my mom.

After another month—I was four months old by then—I was returned to her, and yet again the pattern repeated. This time I was taken to a county shelter. Social workers there told my mom that other people could give me a better life, so she signed away her rights to be my mom.

I was put up for adoption at six months. My adoptive parents had been waiting for five years to get a baby, but by the time they met me, my face was frozen into no expression. I didn't cry or smile or want to be touched. I had given up my Call, which left no possibility for bonding.

Of course, it wasn't personal, but my baby self wanted nothing to do with them. I imagine myself back then as a possum playing dead. Frozen possums may be still, but inside they are full of tension and terror. They're stressed, just surviving. A baby who doesn't cry is a strange thing.

Anyone, baby or adult, who has given up hope for bonding, is in despair. Deeper than depression, too much despair is life threatening. When our natural Calls bring us pain instead of love, no matter how old we are, we shut ourselves down, closing off the world so that nothing can get in, nothing bad or good. We become half dead, barely reachable. That's how I was for a really long time.

My adoptive mom was so anxious about being a good mother, she thought of me as quiet and easy, not strange. Because I wasn't crying, she assumed I was comfortable and that she was doing a good job. But my grandmothers told me later they knew I wasn't easy—something was wrong with me.

My dad had an especially tough time with my aloofness. I wasn't the child he'd dreamed of getting. I didn't smile at him or run into his arms when he got home from work—doing that didn't even occur to me. When I was four years old, he told my mom he was done with being rejected by me, and she could raise me herself.

It's true—I didn't want my dad. But I wouldn't have wanted Superman or Jesus or Yoda either. Well maybe Yoda—he was gentle and wise.

It became super awkward, all three of us living in our house together, my dad not talking to me because he believed I'd rejected him, and it looking to me like he'd rejected me.

My mom hung in there with me, trying for the rest of her life to connect with me, and failing. I appreciate my mom's sense of responsibility and commitment to me, that she hung in there through it all, but bonding never happened. To bond I needed a way to wake up my Call again—of course, back then I didn't even know what a Call was.

When I was a freshman in college taking Psych 101, I learned about Harry Harlow's experiments with baby monkeys who were removed from their mothers. Instead of real moms, they had inanimate cloth and wire monkey moms. These babies preferred the cloth moms to the wire moms, even though the wire moms were the ones with food. Comfort was more important than eating.

Obviously I don't explicitly remember being alone in that crib or being hit by my first mom, but when I learned about these monkeys in class, I felt a chill in my spine, an odd recognition, because our bodies hold implicit memories before we can actually remember things.

Then I heard that these baby monkeys were permanently damaged if they were isolated from their mothers because they missed out on a critical period for attachment. Their brains didn't develop normally, and they didn't know how to socialize with other normal monkeys. Sitting in class, I related to this, too. Socializing had always been frightening for me, even if on the outside I could fake being comfortable.

When I heard that some of these monkeys even died from not having enough of their attachment needs met, I understood. We can die in gradations. I had never really come fully back alive from my infancy even if on the outside I looked like a reasonably normal college freshman. At 18 years old I still hadn't cried or bonded or loved.

Even if we don't learn how to ask for our needs to be met, our Calls still happen, but they curl in on themselves in disguised and dangerous ways. Addictions, isolation, depression and anxiety, lots of conflicts, chronic money problems, procrastination, perfectionism, and suicide attempts are all Calls. I thought I was just messed up, but really I was suffering in a life where my Calls couldn't get out directly. I couldn't ask for help. I didn't even consider it.

Not knowing how to ask for help proved challenging years later when I had babies of my own. My daughters were born 16 months apart, and seeing them so little and helpless overwhelmed me in two ways. First, I saw right in front of me what I must have looked like when I was left alone in the crib and hit and sent from place to place for safety. Second, through answering my babies' Calls with breastfeeding, holding and rocking them, and playing with them, I experienced their easy love for me. They lit up with smiles and a depth of adoration I'd never seen before. I had to navigate the vague but intense pain of my own history and at the same time support their beautiful attachment to me. I needed help with my overwhelm, but I had no words, so I made no clear Call.

Instead, I kept my house clean, lost the baby weight quickly, acted competent, and relied on humor, so people thought I was far more okay than I really was.

I was part of a mom's group, and I was the first one to have a second baby. No one cooked for me or helped me out. They told me I was doing way better than they were with just one baby. We laughed about it, and I was proud of how well I was holding it together in their eyes, but it wasn't true. I was fragile, and it took just a tiny bit of stress to send me to alcohol or ice cream or arguments with my husband. These habits were the only ways I knew how to say, *Help!*

My husband Tom was working full time when our babies were young, and I called him to ask if he could get orange juice on his way home. From his own stress, he angrily said, *I work.* So I hung up and changed our outgoing voicemail: *Hi, you've reached Tom, the only one in the family who works, Pam the freeloader, and Lauren the baby who's raising herself! Please leave a message...beep.* I called all my friends to have them listen to my creative retort and we laughed our asses off, but my deeper Call for help with my overwhelm remained silent. Disguised Calls are so messy.

Because I couldn't handle much more stress than I was chronically living with already, I raised my daughters to be very independent, trying to warn them without saying it that they are on their own in life. *Call and Respond to yourself. Don't lose control of yourself. Don't be vulnerable. People are dangerous.* My kids were being raised by the still-frozen baby. And they got in line: they were polite, did their homework, got good grades, excelled in sports, and got themselves dressed, showered, and sometimes fed, all on their own.

When my daughters were teenagers and my parents were dying, I started seeing Claude, or as I like to call him, The Magic Psychiatrist. I'd seen therapists all my adult life, but Claude had a special set of keys that actually unlocked those inaccessible places from my infancy. He knew if he didn't wake up my authentic Call—not the one asking for orange juice or laughs for my sarcasm, but the frozen Call asking for consistent, loving presence to my deepest pain—I would remain frozen and lonely.

Here's how he did it:

I told Claude that on my deathbed what I would remember most were traveling, taking transformative classes at Esalen in Big Sur, and love affairs in my early 20s with Spike from the Royal Air Force and the architect student from Berkeley who'd played James Taylor songs and treated me like a princess. Those times were the highlights of my life.

Bullshit, Claude said. *That's not your real life. Those aren't your treasures. Your real life, your deepest treasures, are Tom, Lauren, and Sarah (my daughters), your family. You're confused.* He said this more fiercely than usual.

I fought back. *You clearly haven't had much fun in your life, Claude, and I feel sad for you. You should go to Esalen.* I was struggling to stay in control, but I deeply respected him. Being part of my childhood family and my current family had been so stressful for me. I'd never really felt comfortable in a family before—family was where things had gone wrong. My first family had given me away; my second family was something I had survived. My third family now seemed fraught with danger. What if they rejected me, too? What if Tom finally got tired of my trauma and left? What if my kids decided they wanted a different, better mother?

Didn't Claude realize how dangerous family was for me? I was seeing him to get help, and suddenly he was telling me I was on the wrong road. He was pointing me toward *family.*

I left his office with my head spinning. I had been convinced that treasure would only be found *outside* of family.

Intertwined with my fundamental confusion about the value of family were the facts of my lineage. My first mom's grandmother was relinquished by her mom. My first mom's mom was, too. So was my mom, and so was I. We had a lineage of four generations of orphaned girls. *Was abandonment in my DNA? Was I simply, genetically, not cut out to mother? Should I pack a bag and head to Europe or Southeast Asia or anywhere but here?*

I would need lots of help if I was going to move toward my family, help that I couldn't even imagine. I felt like a lobster being asked to willingly climb into a boiling pot of water. Alarm bells were blaring. I didn't know it yet, but these were the ancient alarms, the alarms of my infancy that had shut down my Call in the first place. Claude had his work cut out for him.

He was there on the other end of the phone for five whole years, committed to waking up my ability to Call for help, and he was committed to Responding to my Calls through texts between our sessions. My Calls for help woke up in desperate chunks and sounded like this:

Me: *Hi, I'm in a bind. Both my girls have been very mean and way out of line. Tom doesn't have this problem with them, so he doesn't see it. Right now he and the girls are happily chatting while I'm seething (for a variety of reasons, including shit with my mother). So he's always the soft place to land and I'm the bitch. He thinks I overreact to them and make everything harder, which maybe I do, but I can't help it at this point. Tonight we have to go to their basketball banquet for three hours and I'm absolutely dreading it. I feel agoraphobic and nonfunctional. He thinks my not going would be terrible parenting. I hate him, I hate the girls, I hate my mom, I hate everyone else and have zero to give anyone. I'm afraid not going would reinforce dad is the stable nice one and I'm the crazy bitch.*

Claude's response: *Yes, the sanest thing we can all do, that you want your girls to learn to do, is listen to and respond to their own needs. Simply say, "I'm sorry, I'm feeling really overwhelmed. I am going to stay home." You are not a flake, no matter what anyone says. You will make an impression that you have your limits and are learning to respect them, that you want them to learn to do the same, for you and for themselves.*

That's what I did, and it was good.

Days before my mom's death I texted to Claude: *I had a horrible day. I'm filled with rage and despair and feel disconnected from everyone. Ungrounded, untethered, enraged with my now pitiful mom. Completely uncomfortable in my skin. Having a hard time finding the big person inside. Did visit her without killing her and did make dinner for my family. But fighting with Lauren is causing damage. I hate being alive at this moment, but of course I'm not suicidal. Want to hurt something.*

Claude's response: *I think I get that she is an unresolvable paradox. She gave you almost everything and almost nothing; you are frightened of losing her and filled with resentment of her and want to kill her; you want to talk to her, and you can never talk to her, never could. I recommend screaming into your pillow.*

And I did. But the best part was his explicit understanding of my "unresolvable paradox." I felt deeply seen.

And then, one month later, I began to turn my attention to my family; my truest treasures needed some help.

Claude: *You have been the mother your mother was not able to be. But you have had trouble being the mother you are fully capable of being. You have helped your children far more than you have hurt them, and far more than you were helped. But there are issues to work on, I agree. I think it would be good to have your girls come in with you, one at a time.*

And they did. Claude began doing with the girls, Tom, and our family as a unit what he had been doing with me: unwinding terrible knots, exorcising "ghosts" from our histories and from our ancestors, taking the ghosts off the girls, getting the ghosts out of our family unit, and taking bullshit out of my deepest box of treasure—my family—so that the preciousness of our bonds began to sparkle and matter.

Not only did Claude help me wake up my Call, he helped me support my daughters to wake up their Calls, so they could stop living as if life were so ungenerous and unresponsive.

I started with Lauren. I walked into her room and said, *I'd like to do something nice for you. What do you want?* She looked confused and said, *Nothing.* I said, *No, really—I want to do something you'd like. What do you want?* Annoyed, she said, *Wash my sheets.* So I did, and she laughed a little.

I started anticipating Calls she wasn't making, paying close attention in order to build momentum. If she was running late for school, I'd ask if I could drive her so she wouldn't have to ride her bike. I'd make a special after-school snack to surprise her. I'd stop myself from annoying patterns of interrogation (a disguised Call for her to take on my anxiety about her life).

Sarah was easier. She had lots of Calls just waiting to come out, waiting for me to have more capacity—so I did it with her, too. I showed up at her junior high one day and called her out of class, and we went to the zoo. I tried to listen to her stories without asking annoying questions based on my own anxiety. I bought her favorite smoothie before picking her up from soccer practice. I let her get another guinea pig.

Becoming clever at waking up my daughters' Calls was easier than I thought it would be. I think all our kids are waiting for us to figure this out. Beneath kids' silence and annoyed faces and behind their closed doors and absences from the house, they want parents they can Call to and get truly helpful Responses from.

If you're a parent, you may have a bunch of questions about your own kids and the upsetting things they say and do. *Is this a Call? How is that a Call? How do I respond to him when he's smoking pot, locked in his room every day? How do I show her respect if she doesn't show it to me? I'm human, too, after all.*

For now, stay with Call and Response as being the precious

building blocks of bonding. Calls happening show us that our kids are still hopeful for the bond itself. Calls are essential and healthy. The biggest problem is when the Calls stop. A baby like I was who doesn't cry is in serious trouble—so is a teenager who has profoundly shut you out the way I did to my parents.

Now that my Call is more awake, I can think back to what I needed as a frozen, insulated child. My parents didn't cook, and I needed to be cooked for. My dad's attention was on TV, and I needed his attention on me. My mom was anxious, and I needed her to contain her anxiety so that we could have a conversation that put me in the center, not her. I needed help understanding why doing well in school mattered in a tangible way, and what I'd get out of it, not how it would make my mom feel that she was doing a good job. I needed exercise, therapy, and help with my curly hair.

Most of all, I needed to grieve something I couldn't remember, and I needed something to believe in.

When my kids started to Call again, something unexpected happened—they started to Call a lot. Then they fell apart; they had health crises and emotional crises. They became high maintenance. It was as if the more I Responded well, the more they Called, letting out the stress they'd been carrying. Thank God I was getting help from the newfound magical bonding equation! I had no map for needy kids, so I feared the worst. I worried they'd become dependent adults and live with us forever. Sometimes I'd get really mad at their Calls. Like *For Christ's sake…Really? I've given you the sun today and now you want the moon?* I began to feel the isolated baby I used to be inside of me, still hungry and lonely. Even though I was growing, I was running on fumes trying to give my family more than I had ever come close to receiving.

Changing multigenerational patterns of trauma takes a heroic effort! We have to forge roads that are brand new to us. And they're the roads of our own hidden dreams.

I wanted a mom who kept me and was willing to give me the sun AND the moon in the same day, even though she was exhausted. My children getting what I'd never gotten didn't mean that I hadn't deserved it, too. But to give what I'd never gotten often felt unfair. I was angry that the path of change was so hard, that I didn't have a map and had to figure it out all by myself. It was all insult on top of injury. *This is too unfair. Life is asking too much of me.*

Claude was my lighthouse in the storm of overturning my outdated ways. He gave me hope that investing in my family, even though it seemed unfair, was good for me. I wasn't losing anything by giving to them—I was gaining something.

My strong bond with Claude *was* the foundation that gave me faith in the messy process of turning toward my family.

To forge a new path in parenting takes enormous energy, courage, and stamina. The old voices shout panicked protests: *No! This new pattern of bonding is dangerous! What if they get hurt! What if they die! This is too hard! Let's go back to being independent instead!* But deep down I began to believe the old patterns were deadly and that all the hard work would someday be worth it.

Over time, with Call, Response, Call, Response, Call, Response, the girls' towers of "I'm fine" crumbled, allowing them to become more real, like Velveteen rabbits with their fur all messed up, more authentic and connected.

Now in their early 20s, they have become mostly independent again, but they still Call when they need to. They ask for advice on school and work challenges and come over when they're sick or need support.

They've become good Responders, too. Yesterday, Sarah came over to help Tom create spreadsheets for his business. She had noticed he was getting backlogged and offered her expertise. When we are filled up enough with our own Calls being met, we have energy to give back without falseness or obligation.

My kids are way ahead of me on Calls. Many of mine are still curled in on themselves. When I need help, I still crave beer, ice cream, and Netflix before I even think of asking another human for help. Addiction is a pathway I've traveled for years. I'll be sitting on the couch with a pint of Ben & Jerry's Cherry Garcia, and Tom will ask, *Is something wrong?* I'll say, *Nope, I'm fine.* With the ice cream, I do feel fine for a bit. I'm not easily aware of the barriers I put up, separating myself from the world. I don't want to bother people—they have their own problems going on. And if I ask and they disappoint me, then I'll feel even worse. It's not worth it.

Bonding—both Calling and Responding—requires so much of me. And perhaps it's hard for you, too.

Our culture values independence and being self-made. It's easier to pull self-reliance off when things are going well. But when things go wrong (serious illness, financial stress, divorce, problems with our kids, getting laid off, deaths of loved ones), most of the people I know and the clients I work with aren't comfortable with Calls. They don't want to look weak or make others uncomfortable or be a burden or get vulnerable and then hurt by bad Responses. We as a culture are bad at Responding. We don't know what to say about death and tragedy unless we've gone through it ourselves, and usually only then do we learn to say and do the things we most needed in the hardest times.

I estimate that each client I've seen with a serious illness or loss of a loved one spent at least $1,000 in therapy talking about the hurt they feel from poor Responses from others. When my clients are as vulnerable as they've ever been, and loved ones ask them to see the silver lining in their crisis or avoid addressing what's going on directly, my clients are heartbroken and angry. Poor Responses at critical times can ruin lifelong relationships.

Despite our culture, to feel connected and well we all need to figure out Calls and Responses. Without true Calls we can have no satisfying bonds. And if we don't Respond well to our loved ones' Calls, we will mess up the bonds.

Ultimately, we all need to learn to be comfortable both Calling and Responding in the world. The good news is we can build these practices and a balance between them. Too much Calling as an adult becomes exhausting to others; too much Responding becomes exhausting to ourselves.

Sometimes it takes death to wake up Calls and Responses. On my dad's deathbed, I tried Calling to him for the first time. I said, *Dad, do you like me?* That was the most honest question I had for him. He shot up in bed and said, *Like you? I love you! I admire you! You say you're going to do something and you do it.* I thought, *Holy shit. Thank you.* His Response to my Call quieted one of the terrible messes in me, and I wouldn't have heard those words if I hadn't asked. The last day of his life was my best day with him.

Now when I think of my dad, I feel okay in a way I never did when he was alive. Dying softened him. He dropped into his heart. I picked a good day to make my first adult Call to him.

One of my favorite books is *A Year to Live* by Stephen Levine. He recognized that illness, tragedy, and death create an immediacy and urgency in us to discern what's important in our lives. A veil lifts and we have access to what we really need and how we want to meet and serve the world around us. Without the immediacy of a tragedy, day after day we easily stay in a trance that's just comfortable enough. Our Calls and Responses stay hidden or lazy.

In Levine's program, people form a small group and mark the day of their (fake) death exactly one year in the future. Then they systematically address all the areas of their lives that are important to them as if they literally had only one year left to live. They organize their belongings, make amends, knock things off their bucket lists, clarify their estates, and tell others what they've meant to them. They stop doing what doesn't matter and put their energy into all that does, with focus and urgency.

The group meets throughout the year, forging ahead toward their impending "deaths," sharing stories, supporting and inspiring each other. Then they have their "death" in whatever way they decide. Maybe they lie on the beach or in the forest or in a backyard. Their "death" becomes a rebirth into a new way of living, one with clarity and purpose.

Authentic Calls and Responses become easier to find during a year of "nothing to lose" because "death" is right around the corner.

Sometimes, when we don't know who to Call to yet, we can call on nature and the spiritual realm. One of my favorite stories in Viktor Frankl's book *Man's Search for Meaning* is about a dying woman whom Viktor cared for in the concentration camp. Call and Response are integral to the story:

> *It is a simple story. There is little to tell and it may sound as if I had invented it; but to me it seems like a poem. This young woman knew that she would die in the next few days. But when I talked to her she was cheerful in spite of this knowledge. "I am grateful that fate has hit me so hard," she told me. "In my former life I was spoiled and did not take spiritual accomplishments seriously." Pointing through the window of the hut, she said, "This tree here is the only friend I have in my loneliness." Through that window she could see just one branch of a chestnut tree, and on the branch were two blossoms. "I often talk to this tree," she said to me. I was startled and didn't quite know how to take her words. Was she delirious? Did she have occasional hallucinations? Anxiously I asked her if the tree replied. "Yes." What did it say to her? She answered, "It said to me, 'I am here, I am here, I am life, eternal life.'"* (Viktor Frankl, *Man's Search for Meaning*, p. 69)

Questions for Reflection:

1. With which people in your life do you share the deepest bond? How do Calls and Responses work in those relationships?
2. What are your hidden Calls? What are your hidden Responses? How long have you been hiding them? What has hiding them cost you?
3. Are you better at Calling or Responding? What would it take to get great at both?
4. If you had one year to live, specifically which Calls and Responses would you bring forth?

Actions to Immediately Increase Your Life Force:

1. Ask yourself kindly, *What do I need right now?* Wait for an answer to bubble up. If you're earnest and patient, it will. When it does, even if you don't see a way for your need to be met, knowing what it is and caring about it will help you immediately. You might hear something like, *I'm tired—I need some time off.* Okay, you're depleted and need a break so that you can rest. Now put your hand on your heart, take a deep breath or two and say to yourself silently, *I hear you. You're tired and need some time to rest.* You are honoring your Call simply by giving it space to be known to you. This will move you closer to finding a Response to your Call.

   If your answer is something like, *I need money* or *I need to get off sugar,* this is not your deepest Call. This is a means to your Call. Ask yourself, *What will I feel if I have more money? What will I feel if I get off sugar?* Look for an emotional experience. *I will feel a sense of security if I have more money. I will feel more clear and energetic if I get off sugar.* Then give your deeper Call space to be known by you.
2. Look for an immediate way right now to offer a Response to someone's Call. Check in with a friend who is having a hard

time. Surprise someone with something they love—flowers or a book or a piece of fruit in season. Give a compliment to a stranger. See what happens to your emotional state and energy level after you've Responded. I predict you'll immediately feel more energized and joyful.

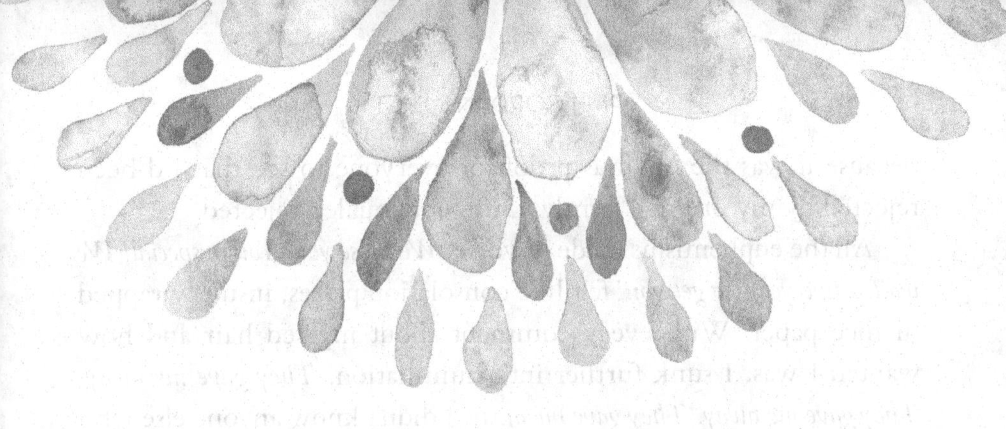

Chapter 2

DIGNITY (VS. HUMILIATION)

We don't earn dignity—we are born with it. Dignity is our inherent worthiness, simply because we are alive. When we honor our dignity, we automatically honor the dignity of others—dignity *always* goes both ways. We recognize the shared light of humanity which is at the basis of our potential to be loving, creative, and wise. Without a sense of dignity, a person is in deep danger.

Where'd you get your red hair? It seemed like this question came at me every time I was in public with my mom. She was four foot ten and had jet-black hair. I was only in fourth grade when I began towering over her, like a monster. We looked like pieces from different jigsaw puzzles—the Alps and Tahiti—and of course, we were.

I was mad about how different I looked—mad was easier than ashamed. I was given away by my first family and I didn't know why, and like any kid I could only imagine it was because something was very wrong with me. I looked strange with my tallness and red hair, bad strange. In my mind, not looking like my parents made me ugly because it was the obvious proof for everyone to see that I'd been rejected by my original family. Different equaled rejected.

All the euphemisms made it worse. *We chose you! You're special! We waited five years to get you!* felt like consolation prizes, insults wrapped in nice paper. With every comment about my red hair and how wanted I was, I sunk further into humiliation. *They gave me away. They gave me away. They gave me away.* I didn't know anyone else who had been given away. I didn't know of anything worse. *Only a really bad baby would be given away. My parents must be so dumb to choose me.* There was no greater sign of failure than being thrown away by your family. I had failed before I could walk.

By age four my dad was already done with me. It was only a matter of time before everyone else would be, too. I pretended I was normal, but I knew people could see the truth—I was an orphan, a misfit, garbage. *They gave me away.*

When I was four, my parents and I went to a spaghetti dinner at my mom's friend's house. I got a stomachache and was sent to the back room to lie down while they finished eating. On the way home, I vomited in the back seat, all over myself and my dad's beloved car. Vomiting was new to me. I didn't even know what vomiting was.

My dad whipped the car over to the side of the road, jumped out, and flung open my door. He yelled, *Jesus Christ! Look at this goddamned mess you made in my car!* My mom just watched from the front seat. Then he took a step back and vomited all over the street, spaghetti chunks splashing on his polished shoes. Enraged, he got back in the driver's seat and flew home, tires screeching. I went to my bed.

Would he come in and hit me? Or even kill me? I wondered. I knew he had a gun next to his bed, and now I'd made him really mad. I was scared to death of him and shivered myself to sleep.

Neither of my parents ever spoke about this again, but something happened to my body that day. My throat, esophagus, and stomach—all the parts involved in vomiting—stopped working for good. For decades I never vomited, even if I got food poisoning or the stomach flu or drank too much at a party. My body just held it in, trying to be good.

Christmas opened the door to the possibility that I mattered. I believed with all my heart that Santa Claus was real and literally aware of me. *He sees you when you're sleeping, he knows when you're awake.* I wondered if I, too, had come from the Island of Misfit Toys; if he cared about them, he must care about me. Santa was the only one who knew my location and the circumstances of my life. He was my only witness; my lifeline to a world that was good.

At Christmas Santa made real contact with me. His gifts in my stocking and under the tree said, *I see you, Pam; you are good and worthy enough for a visit. You get presents, not coal. You're not alone.*

Santa was my introduction to moving out of self-protection, or contraction, and into joy, or expansion. Though I didn't have those words when I was young, on TV I saw his sled flying around the entire world and believed that he cared for everyone, everywhere, equally. He valued all of us, all the cultures, even people on far away islands. His inclusion of everyone, everywhere, all at once, made sense to my heart. Santa was smarter than any real people I knew. He made me feel safe and worthy. On Christmas Eve, I couldn't sleep at all. I was so full of delight that this happy guy would come into my house to care for me.

When I was six, an older neighbor told me Santa was just a story our parents made up. I was stunned. My mom confirmed it, and this harsh reality sent me falling off the scaffolding of a life I was barely holding onto. Life turned gray. If Santa wasn't real, then I was truly alone. I was trapped in a world where I didn't belong and wasn't wanted.

I was so ashamed that I had bought the lie of Santa in the first place that I pulled into myself even more deeply. I became too withdrawn to care or try. After that, each year before Christmas, I snuck into my mom's closet to find all my presents. I carefully unwrapped and rewrapped each one. I was now the one in charge of Christmas; I would not be tricked again.

That same year I was taking a bath on a school night. My hair was full of shampoo, and my mom banged on the closed bathroom door, shouting, *The house is on fire!* I scrambled out of the tub, threw on my robe, and opened the door to a wall of smoke. To my left the furnace was on fire, but I had to get past it to get out the front door. I crawled down the hall against the opposite wall, holding my breath and closing my eyes until I got outside. My parents were already on the porch.

The next thing is what I remembered most for decades, but it was not the most important thing. When I came out the front door, my mom said, *Go back in and get your hair dryer. You're not allowed outside at night with wet hair.* She actually said that! My dad said nothing. He didn't parent me anymore, not on normal days, and not during a fire. I told my mom, *No.* The fire trucks arrived, firefighters put the fire out, and we went to a motel.

The next day in school I told the fire story to my first-grade class. I left out everything except that my house caught on fire and the fire trucks came. I just knew that I didn't want to share what my mom had told me to do.

For decades I told this story to close friends to convey just how ridiculous my mom could be. *Sure, she went to Berkeley and Stanford, but Jesus Christ, when I was six she told me to go back into a burning house to get a hairdryer! Clearly, I had to raise myself!*

During arguments I threw it in my mom's face: *You told me to go into a burning house to get my hairdryer!* And she would say, *Did I really say that? I don't know what I was thinking.* And to be fair, she probably didn't. People can say crazy things in emergencies.

The worst part of this story—the part I couldn't look at directly for so long—didn't dawn on me until just a few years ago: both my parents left me in a burning house and got themselves out first. You and I know that love doesn't do that. Family doesn't do that.

It was after the fire that I got really angry.

One day I marched over to my neighbor's house, and with sticks of chalk I wrote Fuck on each brick on the lower part of their house. *Fuck Fuck Fuck Fuck Fuck Fuck Fuck Fuck Fuck Fuck Fuck Fuck Fuck Fuck Fuck Fuck Fuck Fuck Fuck Fuck Fuck Fuck Fuck Fuck Fuck Fuck Fuck Fuck Fuck Fuck Fuck Fuck Fuck Fuck Fuck Fuck Fuck Fuck Fuck Fuck.* I spelled each *Fuck* correctly, and I never got caught.

Dignity is at the very basis of compassion, justice, and love. Heroes fight for it, and hate abandons it. Dignity is the deepest and most powerful resource we have, and it's there, all the time, waiting for us. We are the ones who become disconnected from it.

Like all of you, I was born with dignity. A baby crying for food is inherently an act of dignity, of value for life itself. *Feed me so I can stay alive.*

The doctor's decision to rescue me three times was a recognition of my inherent worthiness. Why else would he do it—Child Protective Services didn't exist back then. But after I shut down as a baby and started to make meaning of my life as a young child, I lost a sense of having much inherent value at all. If my first family gave me away, if my dad gave up on me, if my parents left me in the fire, wasn't I just a big mistake? Weren't these signs that I was not supposed to be here? Wasn't I essentially bad and worthless?

As I got older, I hoped that I wasn't just a mistake, but believing I shouldn't have been born in the first place was right there, like a shadow following me around. *Why hadn't my first mom just aborted me! When would the wrongness of my life be over already!*

But the thing is, inside we all know the truth—that we do matter, that our lives do hold value—simply because we are alive.

Everything alive, underneath it all, values life—the plant that doesn't get enough water still reaches for the sun and blooms; the runt of the litter still tries to get the milk; a suicidal person still ducks when a frisbee flies near his head. That's what life does—it naturally tries.

So if our environment gives us the message we are bad and unworthy, what happens is we get really mad. A terrible war erupts inside us between the delusion of unworthiness and the truth of dignity. *I want to believe I matter because I do matter, but the world is telling me I don't matter, and I hate that I don't matter to the world, and now I'm starting to hate myself and everyone else and being alive!*

I wasn't at war with my neighbors or the bricks—I was at war with the question of my essential value as a human being. Living with a war like this is exhausting.

In high school I was too full of shame to hang out in the big quad with everyone else, so I hid out in Mr. Voester's math classroom with a few others. There, we did our homework or tried to solve riddles Mr. Voester wrote on the board for us. He was calm and smart, strict and fastidious. Everyone respected him.

Something important happened in his class my sophomore year. Mr. Voester based everyone's grade 40% on exams and 60% on homework. I got A+'s on all of the exams and did zero homework. Obviously, my test scores proved that I had mastered the subject, and I also knew he was a friend of my mom's (who taught at my high school). But I had miscalculated him—he gave me an F in the class!

I acted outraged, but privately I thought it was kind of funny and cool. He wasn't interested in my bullshit; his standards applied to me, just as they applied to everyone else. That meant I was real to him. When people ignored me or let me get away with things, I also got away with not existing. But suddenly, I felt the rub of existence, of mattering. This thrilled me a little.

I had to retake his class my junior year, and this time I did every shred of homework. I became a super student in his class. I even did logic puzzles for extra credit. I'd never worked so hard—mattering to him made me want to try!

Then something even more surprising happened. He was scheduled for foot surgery and would be absent for a week. He asked me if I would teach his class during his absence—while the substitute sat and watched! I felt like a starlet who'd been discovered by a Hollywood director. He prepared me and had confidence in me. I taught the class, and I taught it well.

Mr. Voester shined a light on my inherent worthiness, shielding me from the ongoing intensity of my self-hatred. Under his leadership I gave something of value to others for a whole week. At the time, this was the best experience of my life because I was finally worth something in someone else's eyes.

My mom valued me, too, but I couldn't afford to open myself to her; my buried Calls were so deep and primal that it was too late for that. But I met Mr. Voester as an adolescent, at a time when I needed someone outside of my immediate family to believe I had something to offer the world. I needed a reason to keep living and trying.

Mr. Voester was just being himself, a teacher with standards. What he did for me he did during his entire career; he championed students in math and in integrity. All students. What he gave me in those two years energized me and fortified my spirit for a while. It wasn't a magic bullet—it didn't solve everything—I was too deep in humiliation for that. But the experience buffered me from my internal war getting even worse. Once you truly matter to someone, even if it's just your high school math teacher, no one can take that away from you.

It's a miracle for humiliation to hold on to dignity. Viktor Frankl's life is a testament to this miracle. The Holocaust said to him, *You are hated. Your race is hated. You don't have value. You are worth humiliating and killing. Life would be better without you.*

And yet—he refused to turn against any person or group. This not turning against, this staying *for* every person and for life itself, is the biggest miracle of Viktor Frankl and the basis of all the gifts he offered. If he had turned against others, he would have been lost in an internal war, confused and distracted from his highest potential.

I read Viktor's work before I had any clear understanding about dignity as an inherent aspect of being human and its power as an antidote to the rage that comes from humiliation and self-hatred.

Until I read Viktor, I had never known how to clearly identify or find help for the depth of my own shame. I couldn't adequately describe humiliation to friends or therapists who had never felt ashamed of their very existence. How could they understand what it was like for me if they had no basis of comparison? They just couldn't.

Dignity is as crucial for people as adequate food and clean water. We can live without it for a while, but a lack of dignity costs us dearly and can quickly escalate, becoming life-threatening. The root of hatred, abuse, systemic injustice, suicide, murder, war, and genocide is the absence of dignity.

When a kid is bullied or rejected, they are inundated with messages, subtle and direct, of *There's something wrong with you, You don't belong, You don't matter, The world would be better off without you.* The resulting rage can be directed inward against the self or outward against others, or both.

Again, rage rises when dignity is challenged because in our essence we know the truth—that we are worthy simply because we are alive—and so are others. Any threat to dignity creates tension and opens a door to antisocial behavior, ideologies of hate, and violence.

I don't remember what I was feeling right before I wrote the fucks on the bricks at age six, but I do remember feeling bolstered afterward, as if I'd broken out of prison. But at that point, a line had been drawn—me vs. them—and with division, dignity is lost.

I didn't take my life of crime further than writing on bricks—but I could have. When I see stories about mass shooters, I'm horrified, but I also know that unless the shooter is a sociopath, it takes repetitive, unrelenting rejection and humiliation to push a person so far from valuing humanity that a threshold is crossed and all that's left is rage with a seething, devastating agenda.

The proverb *The child who is not embraced by the village will burn it down to feel its warmth* restores dignity to the criminal or wrongdoer. The crime isn't the first thing; it follows massive rejection and humiliation. There's a context for the setting of the fire, and the whole village is responsible.

Our psychological survival depends on belonging to some community—any community. Our community shows us whether we matter or we don't, whether we are worthy of belonging or we aren't. Our community's love fortifies our sense of dignity. We need to feel a sense of dignity to feel comfortable in our skin and deserving of taking up space on this planet.

What if nearly every suicide and juvenile crime comes from too little love, protection, and generosity from the village?

I'm not condoning crime or blaming families for suicide. But I do remember that dangerous opening in me, where my humiliation could have taken me in either direction—to hope for life or to suicide or prison.

What I most needed was a safe, loving community to remind me of my inherent worthiness, to fortify my life force. This community would be the soil in which I could emerge from the depths of hiding and bring forth the full brightness of my human spirit.

I didn't find a healing community when I was a child, but I'm lucky enough to be part of a healing community for vulnerable children now that I'm an adult. I found it by accident. (Or maybe it found me!)

Four years ago I was sitting in a cafe with a colleague discussing (yawn!) billing practices. Suddenly, a college kid appeared. He said, *Firefly?!* My colleague said, *Slider?!* They embraced, and Disney sparkles surrounded them. *What was that?* I wondered, starting to feel sparkly myself. The answer: the spirit of Camp Kesem.

Camp Kesem is a nationwide community of 144 universities that supports children through and beyond a parent's cancer at free summer camps. Run by passionate and generous college students, Camp Kesem gives children a profound experience of mattering and belonging.

After this coffee with my colleague, I wanted sparkles, too. I applied to volunteer as a mental health professional with Camp Kesem at U.C. Davis. Had I known what awaited me, I would have made a special glittery calendar to count down the days.

Instead, I was in my 52-year-old trance, running on fumes and scrambling to tie up loose ends when I threw old clothes and a novel into a duffel bag. I'm embarrassed to admit I planned to drive my own car to camp instead of riding in the buses with 125 kids and 45 camp counselors. *Vomit? No thanks. Camp songs? Headache.* I changed my mind at the last minute, realizing I needed to enter the experience wholeheartedly. I packed my headache medicine in my lunchbox.

My first moments on duty jolted me into the gravity of the campers' experiences of cancer and loss. Parents shared tragic stories of recent spousal deaths from cancer and worries that their young kids were suffering from fear and depression. In one family a father died the day before camp, and the kids, who were returning campers, chose to go to camp for the comfort it offered.

I was in awe of the high-energy college kids who gave 100% to every task, from bonding with the kids to organizing all the luggage to crossing every logistical detail off the master list so that we could board the buses and start our great adventure. *When was the last time I had that much energy?* I wondered. Their energy continued full throttle throughout the week.

We drove two hours to camp. No one vomited and I didn't get a headache. As I looked at the faces of the apprehensive kids and energetic college leaders, I began to relax and my heart felt stronger, ready to give its very best to the young people working so hard to give theirs.

One day at lunch I was sitting with the 10 year olds. A girl was banging plastic cups on the table. In my head I could hear my dad: *Stop that goddamned racket!* I looked around to see who was going to stop her, but the counselors didn't even look annoyed. Perhaps they realized this girl needed to make some noise. Maybe she'd been keeping herself quiet in a house of grief for months or years and finally needed to explode! Supporting this girl in unwinding in whatever ways she needed was more important than the immediate comfort of the adults at the table. This caught my attention.

In an activity called the Messy Olympics, everyone chose a large container of ketchup, mustard, syrup or shaving cream and ran around a meadow slathering the goop on each other. What a thrill to make an enormous mess and to see that mess outside of oneself rather than holding it in. I watched counselors sit down and let syrup slide into their ears and down their necks, all in the midday sun. *Give me your mess; I'll take it.*

Every night before bed, eight to ten kids gathered with glow sticks for Cabin Chat. Counselors prepared increasingly deep questions to encourage the kids to share about their experiences with a parent's cancer. One night, Moose invited me to join his 14-year-old boys. I was afraid I'd be intruding (*Who is this old lady barging in on our cabin?*), but instead the boys invited me to join their poker game.

When we started the circle, one question was, *How have you changed the most this year?* Most of the boys opened up right away, while others said only a phrase or simply, *Pass.* Moose had the ability to show both vulnerability and strength in his leadership, and I saw the boys quickly trusting him by revealing their private struggles and supporting one another. I smiled all the way back to my cabin.

After a week of games, adventures, campfires, and deep sharing, we rolled back into Davis wearing our dirty tie-dyed shirts, smiling as brightly as we ever had before. The kids returned stronger, more connected, more hopeful. And so did I.

Kesem means "magic" in Hebrew, and the culture at Camp Kesem is magical in its inclusiveness and commitment to meeting everyone—children, college counselors, and professional staff—with unwavering regard. The week at camp is an infusion of dignity itself. We can say the wrong things, sing and dance "badly," cry, tell embarrassing stories, and be loud, silly, smelly, dirty, and just our plain old selves. In a few short days, the campers drop their facades, begin unwinding their pain, and realize they are not alone. Their confidence returns, and their faith in life itself is strengthened. The Kesem magic is so powerful it lasts all year.

What a relief it would have been to go to a camp like this when I was a child. To share pain and joy with others in a supportive community would have fortified my frightened and tired spirit. To see hundreds of vulnerable kids receiving this gift inspires me. As I sit in the forest at camp, the little me who got left by her first family and left in the fire sits there, too, finally safe and worthy like everyone else.

Dignity and resilience are essentially connected. Dignity has an answer for any circumstance that might separate you from others. Dignity finds a way to say, *You matter; you belong here; you are worthy; and so am I.*

I marvel that Viktor gained his freedom and resumed his life in Austria, in a mixed neighborhood—Jews and Nazis together. Miraculously, he retained his dignity and refused to turn against anyone. I'm sure this saved him and prepared him to build a new life for himself, a life based largely in serving others. He moved forward with self-respect and with respect for others because, of course, these go hand in hand.

I'm doing the same. My family gave me away, my parents left me in a burning house—and yet, I inherently matter anyway. I have value to offer the world. And so do you.

Questions for Reflection:

1. Who are the strangers and friends who have shown you that they value you when you were the most compromised, when your self-doubt or shame dominated you?
2. Share a story about how someone helped to remind you of your sense of worthiness when you forgot.
3. What kinds of things have you done for others, especially vulnerable children, that might have seemed small but may have significantly changed their lives?
4. What are more ways you can give to others who are vulnerable, lost, or hopeless? Could a practice of offering dignity be integrated into your life? Into your family's life?

Actions to Immediately Increase Your Life Force:

1. Make a list of three times you've been shown dignity in your life. Feel the impact of these experiences and silently say, *Thank you.*
2. Remind yourself that dignity is always your companion simply because you are alive. It never shrinks or leaves, no matter what bad things you've done or have been done to you. Ask it for help. "Call" to it. Choose a favorite color to represent dignity and feel it move into you like light, filling you from head to toe. Walk around experiencing it, knowing it is true.

Chapter 3

DIRECT EXPERIENCE (VS. SURVIVAL BRAIN)

We all live with self-limiting beliefs. We create them when we are very young. They become established in us through repeated experiences within our families and in the larger world. They sound like *I'm unloveable, I'm not enough, I don't belong, I'm stupid, I'm ugly.* Once we create them, we begin reinforcing them with "evidence." *See, the teacher never calls on me . . . I really am stupid.* The "evidence" we collect sears these beliefs about ourselves into our nervous systems.

All of our self-limiting beliefs were formed in the context of intense emotions. It took an emotionally charged situation to create a sustainable belief about our true place in the world. When you were four, if your dad was angry and your mom was fragile, it might have made sense for you, in the context of heightened fear, to decide to shut up and not rock the boat. If your family was down and desperate, it might have made sense for you, in the context of heightened worry, to become a comedian or an overachiever to lift them up. In our childhoods during stress, the beliefs we form and the decisions that arise from them aim to save us and our world.

Think about me alone all day in that crib and about the fact that when my mother finally showed up, she hurt me when I cried.

Like any animal, I saved myself by shutting myself down. Trying to change deep-seated beliefs as adults rings all the alarm bells. Since my baby decision to stop crying was wired into my nervous system in the context of terror, I still struggle to cry 54 years later.

When my house caught on fire, I formed a deep-seated belief that I had to protect myself because no one else was going to do it. This belief even informed the way I raised my own kids. Self-limiting beliefs can define family cultures for generations!

Limiting beliefs are not hard to identify. If you look at any current problems in your life and refuse to blame anything outside of yourself; if you follow your thoughts and feelings down, down, down, you will discover what you deeply believe about yourself. It can look like this:

My boss treats me like shit. Now tune in to the sensations in your body, perhaps a tightness in the chest, a pit in the stomach (stay with it) . . . *I feel like shit. How long have I felt this way?* Be patient; if you genuinely ask yourself something, the answers will come. *Oh yeah, the way my mom always seemed to prefer my sister. She was her favorite. I was never good enough.* There it is, a core self-limiting belief.

What do we do about self-limiting beliefs? First I'll tell you what doesn't help: blaming them on anything outside yourself, ruminating and talking habitually about them, and simply reading self-help books to try to change them. Here's why:

To heal, we are not looking for a solution; we are looking for an experience.

Einstein was right when he said we can't solve our problems using the same thinking we used when we created them in the first place. Most of our thoughts happen automatically and are based in the past. They're not very smart; in fact, most of our thoughts just stress us out. We can't even believe a lot of what we think. To heal we need something deeper than thoughts—a new experience.

I started understanding what it takes to heal from my former therapist, Jim. He was a strict Gestalt therapist; he would only tolerate sessions grounded in the present moment. He didn't want to hear about my week or my childhood. He wanted to talk about Right

Now. I tried to sneak the past in, but he wouldn't have it. *What do you notice right now? What sensations are you aware of in your body? What's the figure?* (The figure was the thing that had my attention in the present moment—the person upsetting me or the ache in my stomach.)

Getting into the present moment felt like a disruption to all the important stuff I wanted to talk about in therapy. *Wasn't this my hour? After all, I was the one paying him; didn't I have a say?* I thought I needed him to validate my side in arguments with my husband and how wrong my dad had been to bail on me. The present moment felt like an empty space where nothing that mattered existed. The present moment felt like a distraction from everything I thought I needed. The present moment was a useless waste of time, a lonely void. *Who would pay money to explore the present moment?*

What I didn't know yet was that I was in the habit of using my drama and limiting beliefs to prop myself up so that I didn't sink into more difficult emotions—deep despair and debilitating shame. I was addicted to the biochemical charge I got from anger; it protected my fragile ego (*How dare my dad ignore my kids just like he ignored me!*). Anxiety got me up in the morning—I didn't want to become nonfunctional and mentally ill like my first mom. *What if I have her genes? What if one day I just can't get out of bed and have to be hospitalized?*

The habits of anger and anxiety were pillars for my functioning and "self-respect." I couldn't imagine a life without them. And I had nothing to replace them with anyway.

If you follow the work of psychologist Rick Hanson, Ph.D., author of *Buddha's Brain* and *Hardwiring Happiness,* you already know that our brains have a negativity bias that assumes danger. This defensive system is hardwired into our brains and is not easily controlled. A piece of rope looks like a snake. A shadow looks like an axe murderer. We react more strongly to danger than we do to positive or neutral events. And our brains hold on to negative experiences like Velcro while positive experiences slide off like Teflon. If 99 people love your presentation and one person criticizes it, you will obsess about that one person's remarks. As unpleasant as this is, the negativity bias is what helped our species stay alive for millions of years.

The negativity bias shouts at us, *Since one time there was a tiger behind a tree, there could be a tiger behind every single tree from now on; every tree is dangerous! And if you tripped while running away from the tiger that could have been there, you could trip every time you run away from now on! And if no one was there to help you get up from tripping that first time, no one may ever be there to help you the next time! And if someone is mad at you, you might get kicked out of the tribe, and that would be the end of you!* Our negativity bias alerts us to one possible danger after another and overgeneralizes danger when there is no danger at all.

Even when we are not in real or imagined danger, when we are just hanging out on the couch doing nothing, the Default Mode Network of the brain is active. This network is constantly reviewing who we are and how we're doing, based only on past information, previously established coping strategies, and existing narratives. Everything comes to us through the filter of our interpretations of the past. This network is based in self-reference, in *Me, Me, Me,* and is correlated with unhappiness.

We wake up in the morning, and our Default Network is off and running. It might sound like this: *I have to call John back ASAP. I completely forgot and he's gonna be mad. And the kitchen is a disaster. What are my kids' friends gonna think? We have no food, and I can't wear that outfit again but nothing else is clean. When is the weekend going to get here?* On and on it goes, torturing us with stressful, self-centered thought patterns.

Even when we *are* able to enjoy ourselves in the present moment, the Default Network kicks in at the first sign of stress. It provides us with familiar strategies and pathways that are already known to work: tensing our muscles, isolating ourselves, telling someone off, overeating, scrolling through social media. These patterns are like an outdated operating system, but we have the capacity to build a new one. Moment by moment we can learn to release ourselves from the prison of the past.

We have an entirely different network in our brains—cue the happy music!—called the Direct Experience Network. It kicks in when we explore something new in the present moment. We see a beautiful sunset or a cute dog or a have a friendly interaction with a stranger or solve a puzzle, and all our attention moves to what's immediately happening *right now.*

Here's the kicker: **We can't heal in the Default Network—we can only heal in our Direct Experience!** We need new information and new experiences in the present moment to activate new neural pathways.

These two networks are on separate train tracks. We can't be in both networks at the same time. We have to hop tracks to move from one to the other. It comes down to this: we are either reinforcing old negative patterns in our Default Network, or we're building new patterns through Direct Experience!

If a client comes into my office and wants to talk for 50 minutes straight about all the terrible ways her husband is just like her dad, if she is talking into a vacuum because she's not even aware that I'm with her in the room, she will walk out at the end of the session unchanged and actually worse because she's reinforced her Default Network. Now the painful pattern is even stronger.

The only way to include the past in therapy is if something brand new happens with the old material right now in the therapy session. When I relate to a client's past or Default Network in a brand-new way in the present moment, when I surprise the client with a new possibility in their old story, then something valuable and healing can happen in the session. Their brain will change for the better.

For example, if a client has always wanted to be a writer but was shamed for it in her family, it might make sense to talk about how she was shamed. But if the stories of shaming in the family have been told and are worn out and have become habits—I might try something to more effectively help her. I'll ask her to tell me more about what kinds of things she wants to write. I'll get excited with her—because dreams from the soul are always exciting!

As she begins to brighten and become more animated in her sharing, I might ask her to stand up on the chair and tell me her ideas with greater volume and enthusiasm (*In my shoes?? . . . Yes! In your shoes!!*). Now we are doing something brand new, with intense emotions—exuberance, joy, hope—to give her a powerful experience in her Direct Experience Network, which will change her brain. If she comes in the next week saying she finally was able to write a short story, I will not be surprised because, again, it is through experience, not solutions, that we grow and transform.

Leaving the Default Network behind as much as possible in favor of Direct Experience, whether in therapy or on our own, takes courage and grit. It requires vigilance against our old, well-worn habits because they are deeply embedded in us and ready to pull us into the old traps at any moment.

Elizabeth Gilbert said, *Turn your face stubbornly to the light, and keep it there.* Like a sunflower that turns to follow the light, we can choose where we put our focus at any moment. Directing our focus is within our control, not in the control of the world outside of us. It's a practice, a discipline we must cultivate. It's the key to changing our brains!

Viktor understood this:

> *The last of the human freedoms: to choose one's attitude in any given set of circumstances, to choose one's own way. And there were always choices to make. Every day, every hour offered the opportunity to make a decision, a decision which determined whether you would or would not submit to those powers which threatened to rob you of your very self, your inner freedom; which determined whether or not you become the plaything to circumstance, renouncing freedom*

> *and dignity.* (Viktor Frankl, *Man's Search for Ultimate Freedom,* p. 66)

Any situation is always full of possibilities, but when our negativity bias and all the "evidence" we see tricks us into thinking things are bad or hopeless, we become lost. A trip to the grocery store could become a public humiliation if I run into someone who hates me. If my husband tailgates in freeway traffic, I could die in a grizzly car accident. If he and I are having an argument, we might be headed for divorce! My negativity bias, like yours, is on high alert, and turns belonging into banishment, normality into catastrophe, and wholeness into brokenness.

My therapist Jim explained to me that the fastest way out of the negative story is through our senses, particularly through our eyes. We can be in our Default Network, self-centered and imagining something upsetting, and if we then truly inhabit our eyes and notice what they're looking at right in front of us, the default story stops.

I remember the first time I practiced this. Tom and I had an explosive argument right before I headed to work. I was driving down a major boulevard in Davis—probably to work with a married couple!—and my Default Network was going crazy. *I'm done with him. Between clients, I'm gonna look on Craigslist to find an apartment to move into. That was bullshit. Who does he think he is!*

But I remembered what Jim said and practiced inhabiting my eyes between my mental tirades. My eyes found the red and orange leaves dropping from the valley oak trees lining the road. *Whoa! Look at the colors! So beautiful! So many shades of red and orange!*

Then I slipped right back into my Default Network. *I'm definitely going to remember those two things he said. I'm gonna write them down so I never forget.*

Then I remembered to go back to my eyes. *Whoa, look at that leaf! Just think, it's been on that tree for months. I've driven by that leaf so many times, and now I just witnessed that leaf falling from the tree. It's actually a miracle!*

Back and forth I went, Default to Direct Experience, rage to autumn beauty, my physiology following suit—charged to relaxed. Sometimes we think we have to wait for a mood to pass or for the outside world to change for us, but that's not true.

Tony Robbins says, *Where focus goes, energy flows.* I am in charge of my focus, and you are in charge of yours. Changing our focus is a practice, a new muscle to build. Even if the autumn leaves captured my attention for only three seconds at a time, that was three seconds of changing the channel from fight or flight—the sky is falling and I'm an orphan in a shit show—to the ecstasy of really being present and part of this beautiful life.

It's the act of shifting your attention INTO your Direct Experience that builds the "muscle" you need to be in charge of where you focus. The most powerful part is knowing that shifting your focus is 100% in your hands. Once you realize you're in control of your focus, you can start putting your energy into making your life significantly more empowered and meaningful.

Most of us therapists are "nice" and let clients talk WAY too long before stepping in to redirect a diatribe about the same old thing. I've scotch-taped amusing therapy cartoons from the *New Yorker* on my office wall. In my favorite, a Freud-like therapist in a chair speaks to a male client on the couch. The caption reads, *Tell me about your mother again, this time in a slow, sultry falsetto.*

Clients are passionate about their default stories, and they want to be listened to and validated because they don't know a better way to heal. Their Default Network wants the therapist to fall in the trap and say, *Oh, that sounds very hard, so upsetting* (hand on heart), *tell me more about how you felt when that mean bird chose YOUR head to shit on in 1985, picked YOU to humiliate.* I'm not trying to be mean. I've been on both sides of this equation—the therapist and the client. The

Default Network is a major impediment to the healing process and very hard to disrupt!

Some clients believe that if they've paid a therapist a bunch of money for 50 minutes, they *own* those 50 minutes and can do anything they want. It's *their* hour. I call this kind of therapy "emotional prostitution," and like every therapist I know, I've done it, either because I don't want the client to be mad at me or because I'm tired and don't have the energy to fight the intensity of the Default Network. It takes a lot of energy and courage from both the therapist and the client to move from old, patterned stories to the present moment.

When a client jumps into their Default Network, the atmosphere in the therapy room changes; it gets tight, tense, rigid. The story condenses into what Martin Seligman, positive psychologist, called the "Three P's": Personal (the problem is me), Permanence (the problem will last forever), and Pervasiveness (the bad situation exists everywhere in my life). A client needs help to hop the tracks into the present moment.

Fifteen-minute museum therapy would be far more effective than sitting on a couch, folded at the hips, and talking for 50 minutes about how your jerk of a husband will never change or how your mother just won't stop undermining you or how your 14-year-old son is definitely a narcissist and destined for a terrible future. I've done all of that, and it doesn't work.

I want you to save time, money, and unnecessary pain! So instead, let's walk around a museum together and look at some art, our bodies upright, our breath expanding as we walk together. We're together in the present moment, curious about the life that is right here right in front of us. Show me which scenes, which colors and contours, your eyes like most.

But that's not what I need! your Default Network says. *I need you to tell me what to say to my son when he says "Go to hell!" and comes home after curfew.*

I'll tell you what to do in the parking lot as we walk to the entrance of the museum. *Say, "Ouch" and take away his car keys. Now let's go look at art. Shall we get an espresso first?*

But my husband! you say. *His tone of voice. He won't change. In twenty years. He's just like my father.*

My chest tightens because I, too, know how to go to where you are, into the hellish story, stuck in the victim place with no clear answer or course of action.

That's how it is with our minds. The victim stories muck us up, bind us in chains. Fifteen minutes at the museum is a glorious sip of freedom. A short walk reminds us that we can move in this direction or that. A look at colors and shapes is tonic for our tired spirits. A smile with a trusted other is stabilizing to a heart thirsty for connection.

Don't waste your money or time recycling terrible stories unless they lead to something new happening in the present moment. Find a therapist who will infuse your system with what is here and alive. Resuscitate yourself with Direct Experiences of art, nature, movement and love.

In his TED Talk, neuroscientist Jaak Panksepp, Ph.D. said one of our most threatening hardwired emotional systems is the "Panic/Grief" system that babies experience when a bond with a parent is severed. When this loss is sustained over time, both animals and humans enter a downward spiral of psychological depletion. We lose motivation for finding pleasure, our curiosity is dulled, and we stop caring.

The bridge out of this is Curiosity, what Panksepp calls it the "Seeking System," which is hardwired in us. Curiosity is a shift of attention into the present moment. Imagine an owl perched in a tree looking for prey on the ground, cocking her head to observe the landscape more closely. Curiosity is a bridge to a new possibility; it is the way out of "Panic/Grief," despair, and depression.

To feel better at any moment, step one is to get curious about what is right in front of you. *What kind of flower is that? I wonder where that woman across the street is going? Who designed this building?* At first the answers are unimportant because simply asking a question will wake up the hardwired, emotional Seeking System in the body and increase well-being almost immediately.

Often, though, one question isn't enough. Two or three are much more powerful. With the first question, *What kind of flower is that,* I can stay on the fence: maybe I care and maybe I don't. Maybe I'll go right back to my misery. A second or even third question takes a giant step further toward "the other," whatever that is, and away from our own chattering mind of despair. *Who planted that flower? What inspired them to choose that particular type of flower? How were they feeling when they planted it?* Curiosity leads us "out of the woods" into the possibilities of playfulness and joy.

My friend Melody's father, Harris Meisel, was a physician, artist, musician, and poet, who built his life on a practice of wonder—or in his words, *eyes that see.* Not only did he establish the Cottage Rehabilitation Hospital in Santa Barbara, which serves patients with head and spinal cord injury, he incorporated art and music into their healing, and he showcased their artwork in the hospital hallways. He knew that art would nourish their eyes and fortify their spirits as they did the hard work of recovering.

After his death, Melody shared that her father asked not one, but at least two questions as a practice of curiosity. When his eyes found something of interest, he stayed with it, allowing his sense of wonder to take root. He then might draw a sketch or jot down an inspiration or write a short, delightful poem for a stranger. At home he carved fruit into whimsical animals and played his guitar down the hallway at night, singing his kids to sleep. His devotion to Direct Experience was clear.

The people around Dr. Meisel benefitted because Direct Experience is not only fortifying, it is contagious! Surely at least two questions are involved in carving an animal out of a piece of fruit! Which fruit? Which animal? Where should its head be? Once we are thinking about where to carve the head, then we begin to visualize the body, the legs, and the tail, too. All we need now is a knife to start carving a bird from a pear.

Having "eyes that see" takes practice. In our worst moments, it's really difficult to care about anything outside of our desperate ruminations. But as we keep at it, every time we turn our focus away from stress, even momentarily, to inhabit our eyes in the present moment and become curious, we build vital new neural pathways, changing our brains.

When my friend Anne Heffron and I facilitate retreats, we start explaining the limitations of the Default Network and the power of Direct Experience on the first day. We put participants in pairs and send them on a special secret mission. They go outside and find their partner a perfect leaf as a gift. They have to inhabit their eyes, looking for just the right one. Then they return and gift them to each other with an explanation of why it was chosen just for them.

As with my fantasy of "Fifteen Minute Museum Therapy," the benefits of this leaf activity happen quickly. Each participant gets a substantial (20 minute) break from their Default Network dominating them, and they enjoy the experience of offering and receiving kindness from a stranger. *I got you this leaf because it's bold and colorful, like you are. There's a broken edge here, kind of what's happening in your life, but that doesn't change the beauty of it!* As soon as this activity is complete, Anne and I see a roomful of bright eyes, big smiles, open bodies, and often tears. It's so simple and yet so meaningful. People tell us months later that they still have their cherished leaf.

The power of the present moment is under-utilized in healing and growing, both in and out of the therapy session. "Right now" is the only place we can heal and grow, and it is here all the time, ready to offer us countless chances to shift our focus into curiosity and new possibilities.

Questions for Reflection:

1. What has your habit of the Default Mode Network cost you? What time, sense of well-being, intimacy, and joy have been stolen by its power?
2. What rituals can you put in place to spend more time in the here and now, in what some people call the "generous present moment?"
3. What would your life be like in a week, a month, a year if you diligently practiced spending more time in your Direct Experience? Be specific.
4. Who in your life could join you in the practice of increasing your Direct Experience? Which of your loved ones are most open to growth?

Actions to Immediately Increase Your Life Force:

1. Inhabit your eyes right now and let them find something they want to look at. Move into curiosity by silently asking two questions about it, and then two more.
2. Find a Direct Experience accountability buddy. Push each other to spend more time in the Direct Experience rather than in the Default Network. Enjoy hearing each others' stories of rescue missions from old patterns and discovery of beautiful things right here and now!

Chapter 4

ATTITUDE, OUR LAST FREEDOM
(VS. VICTIMHOOD)

According to Albert Einstein, the most important question we can ask ourselves is whether we believe the universe is hostile or friendly. Your answer to this question reflects the core positioning of your life.

Until I was 46, I lived in a hostile universe. *Given away? Adopted by those people? No witnesses to my pain?* It was definitely a hostile universe. And somewhere around the time of the furnace fire and writing the fucks on bricks, I had become hostile as well. Hostile eyes see evidence of hostility; hostile ears hear evidence of hostility. Our core positioning is self-perpetuating. If you are more psychologically intact than I was, you might flip-flop, depending on how things are going. A promotion? Friendly universe. A messy divorce? Hostile universe.

The universe isn't the one that changes, though, right? We do.

Some people believe it's a betrayal to think of the universe as friendly when so many terrible things are going on in the world. The political landscape, global warming, egregious acts—how could a moral person possibly think of the universe as friendly in the face of it all?

The ability to hold a paradox—seemingly conflicting positions—is a hallmark of mental health. It is possible to love someone who does something unthinkable. I've worked with parents whose kids have killed themselves or committed a terrible crime against others. Part of these parents' grieving process is finding a way to give themselves permission to honor their deep love for their child, while at the same time being so very angry at what they did: a paradox, but both are true.

My challenge in imagining that the universe was friendly was having to accept that this "friendly" universe allowed me to suffer so greatly from my very first days. Would believing the universe was friendly mean I was letting everyone off the hook? Wouldn't such a belief be the ultimate betrayal of myself?

That's where Viktor helped me again, in a very important way. He directly addressed my dark and crucial questions: *Why shouldn't I give up on life? Didn't my circumstances define me? Hadn't they shaped my life and damaged my brain forever? What power did I have in the face of it all?* The thought of fighting for a better life exhausted me. But then I read this:

> *There were always choices to make. Every day, every hour, offered the opportunity to make a decision, a decision which determined whether you would or would not submit to those powers which threatened to rob you of your very self, your inner freedom; which determined whether or not you would become the plaything of circumstance, renouncing freedom and dignity to become molded into the form of the typical inmate.* (Viktor Frankl, *Man's Search for Meaning*, p. 66)

And this:

> *In the final analysis it becomes clear that the sort of person the prisoner became was the result of an inner decision,*

> *and not the result of camp influences alone.* (Viktor Frankl, *Man's Search for Meaning,* p. 66)

I was trapped in seeing the world through my circumstances—that I was a victim and nothing more. Viktor deliberately and systematically said there was something "more." What he spelled out addressed my fundamental reluctance to move toward life when I felt so forsaken by my circumstances. He articulated the reason I should hang in there. *There is more to me than my circumstances. I still have power despite my circumstances.* These were brand new thoughts.

Viktor was willing to stay invested in a world that had treated him with cold hatred. He didn't let bitterness overtake and finish him, but instead found meaning in his own suffering and in the suffering of others. He didn't define his life by loss, humiliation, and unfairness, but in terms of a search for meaning. He believed in the grace of life itself even in the face of human depravity.

In fact, the original title of his book *Man's Search for Meaning* was *Say Yes to Life!*

After the Holocaust, during which he lost his pregnant wife, his parents, and his siblings (except for one sister), Viktor remarried and had a daughter and grandchildren. He climbed mountains, wrote, traveled, and spoke about the power accessible to all of us to find meaning regardless of circumstances—to choose our attitude toward suffering no matter what.

I sometimes think, *Yeah, but he wasn't adopted. As his brain was forming the most, he was intact, with his mom and dad, safe and loved. He was kept.*

Survivors of genocide could say, *Yeah, but you were hungry only for parts of six months. You were rescued by the system, not debased and killed off by the system.*

But such a dialogue misses the point. It is unavoidable that some people have it better than others. Yet meaning is available to even the most destitute. Meaning does not "fix" conditions. We live with meaning despite conditions, and sometimes because of them. Regardless of our circumstances, we all have the power to choose the way we approach the limitations of our lives. This final freedom belongs to all of us.

Until later in life, I didn't want to abandon my grievances. I thought they were my deepest truths. I didn't realize they were actually a prison and a distortion of life itself.

Before I realized I had any choices beyond being entrenched in victimhood, I was deeply immobile. I looked like a soccer mom with a white minivan and clothes from J.Crew, but under my suburban disguise I felt frozen and stuck between worlds—between life and death. I was middle-aged and had kids by then! Of course I loved them and would never have wanted to do anything close to leaving them, as my mother had done to me. But I lived on the precarious rim of a frightening black hole. It wouldn't take a lot for me to fall in.

Good times and successes were fleeting and dependent on things outside of me going well. I thought a perfect cup of coffee, my kids being happy, or a fun weekend trip with a friend were matters of good luck and had little to do with my own agency. Inside I was fragile, waiting for the other shoe to drop.

Any relationship problem knocked me into a dangerous state of desperation because in my mind, any conflict harkened back to the first conflict—being given away by my family, having no say about it, feeling rage at "them," and suffering with shame that I must be bad to the bone. Of course I couldn't fight for my side as a baby, but my argument was in there. It sat in my guts, vigilant, ready to rise and unleash itself in any current situation that resembled the old abandonment. A rude checker at the grocery store could lead to hours of alternating revenge fantasies and self-loathing.

The worst thing—a bad argument with my husband—sent my brain spinning into suicidal thoughts. He always wanted space in our conflicts, and I became the madwoman who couldn't cope or leave him alone until the conflict was thoroughly worked out. Space meant "impending doom" to my old brain. So once he made his boundaries crystal clear, I lay on the downstairs sofa, feeling like that baby in a crib, forsaken. *Life hates me. I hate life. Why am I here? I just want to be dead.*

These feelings didn't come from some kind of strategic thinking, such as *The world would be better off without me.* These feelings came from my belly—an anguish that rose up like a geyser and decimated my ability to think. These were memories in my body of too much need, too little love, too much pain, nowhere to find relief. The enormous pain now in my whole body felt as if an alien had overtaken me. But I knew that alien—she was me as a baby, and I was now feeling all the things I couldn't afford to feel when I was so young.

I did my best to talk to the baby, to be her witness. I'd put one hand on my belly and the other on my heart and look up at the ceiling, wide-eyed at the magnitude of my pain. *Could a baby feel something this intense and awful? Could feelings like this kill a baby? Could a baby die from need?*

I'd go driving around, sometimes at 3 a.m., running away from Tom, the kids, the house, and the whole town—feeling desperate, alone, and enraged. Once I drove to my parents' house and parked outside on the street. Their living room light was on, and I knew my insomniac dad was awake. I imagined knocking on the door and asking him to hold me; but I couldn't risk it, so I just sat there, parked near his light.

I only told Tom and close friends how bad it got, but living on this edge, trying to avoid inevitably falling in the hole, was my way of life. Even though I saw great therapists over the years, I couldn't cry with any of them. I was still too frozen to Call for the help I needed. When clients came into my office and cried the whole session, I deeply admired and envied them. *How are they able to do this? They have problems, but they are actually much more intact than I am,* I'd think.

I had been working with my therapist Jim for four years, loving him and our work together, when we had an argument. In a small, weekly consultation group, I challenged him about a situation concerning his answering service. He said, *Fuck you.* A guy next to me told Jim he didn't like the way he'd spoken to me. Jim said, *Fuck you, too. Group is over.*

I tried to work it out with him, but he said, *You have an abandonment and betrayal problem.* I said, *You're right, I do. But you have something, too.* He said, *Nope, it's all you.* (Just what my dad might have said.) I lost trust in Jim and couldn't continue to work with him. I vacillated for two years between the anguished rage of *He's bad* and the equally anguished shame of *I'm bad.* I felt ashamed that many of my friends and colleagues still worked with him. *Just like with my first family, I must be the problem,* I thought.

Two years later, in November 2009, Jim jumped off a bridge to his death.

He had been of guru status in our area: the therapist for therapists; the one who could open doors that other therapists couldn't even see. And he really was that guy.

Just how innovative and brilliant he was is apparent from some dream work he did with me. From the time I was a child, I'd had a recurring dream that bad guys were after me. They were in my house, hiding in closets and attics. They were outside my house, breaking in through windows. They shape-shifted; they could be *anywhere,* and I was their target.

While I was working with Jim, I had a dream I was in a huge movie theater. The lights hadn't dimmed yet but the audience was seated. Two guys stood up across the room and pointed machine guns straight at me. (Notice the hostile universe in these dreams?)

I told Jim about this dream, and he asked, *Have they ever killed you?*

No, I always wake up first.

Let's have them kill you and see what happens, he continued.

Um . . . okay, I said, frightened but interested.

He positioned himself across the room and pretended to shoot me dead with a machine gun. I went from sitting to slumping down, to sliding onto the floor and dying. He waited. I lay there, imagining bleeding out, heart and breath stopping, becoming still. I started to feel deeply relieved. I was done! It was over! Now I was in the dirt, seeping into the soil. The bugs came in, eating me, composting me, and I felt joyful ease. Dying was great! Peaceful! No big deal!

I never had that dream again. Jim had cured me.

The day we heard he'd died, I watched my friends collapse in shock and cry. Some looked for an explanation that protected his brilliance: *The jump was a heroic act in which he courageously chose his freedom*. I didn't believe it.

Part of me was jealous. Jim was free now, soon to be dissolving into the earth, decomposing. Done with it all. When would I have my turn? Just being alive felt like life was against me. Maybe he *was* brilliant in his suicide; maybe some of us *should* follow him.

Four days after Jim's suicide, I took a class at Esalen in Big Sur, and a chance encounter began the shift in my relationship with death and life. This is how I began to finally get off the fence to choose life wholeheartedly.

The class was called *Healing the Healer,* and on the first night we had to introduce ourselves and say what we wanted out of the weekend. I told the room that my former therapist had just killed himself, and I couldn't breathe deeply. My only goal for the weekend was to find my breath.

Then we had to pair up with someone to do a class activity. I partnered with Peter, an AIDS doctor. He told me that when he was a baby, his dad had jumped to his death from a building in New York. Peter's relatives had spoken of his dad's death as "an accident."

When Peter began working with AIDS patients in the 80s, it became clear to him over time that his father's death was no accident—his father had chosen death. Peter also realized it was no accident that his own life's work had become trying to save men (mostly young men) from death.

Peter's dad had chosen to leave him, and all his relatives had covered it up. He'd had a rough time, but he didn't stay frozen like me. He excelled at directing an AIDS clinic, raised a family, did community service, studied great thinkers, read poetry, learned to dance, facilitated grief groups with the protégés of Elisabeth Kubler-Ross, wrote a book, spoke around the world, and took care of his mother. He wasn't a "guru" like Jim, but a man who loved life despite profound, personal loss.

I, too, was successful, had a family, and did interesting things. But deep down, Peter and I were different. Peter lived like the world was his oyster, like he was invited to the "party" of life, like he fundamentally belonged. But I hid out largely rejecting life because it felt like life itself had rejected me.

That weekend I realized that inside of me I had both men—a Jim and a Peter. I had been living on the fence, not knowing whether to choose life, like Peter, or death, like Jim. I didn't know how to make the choice, or for what reasons. Viktor often quoted Nietzsche, who said that a person can figure out how to live as long as they have a why. I had never found a why to commit to either side—life or death.

A month later an email arrived from Peter. The subject line told me it was a link to the California AIDS Ride. Each year 3,000 cyclists ride 545 miles down the coast, from San Francisco to Los Angeles, to raise millions of dollars for people living with HIV/AIDS. They do this to honor loved ones and to give support to people they will never meet. It took me an entire month to open that email.

I'm not an athlete. I lasted five minutes at basketball tryouts in high school; as soon as we started line drills, I was out. I just walked right out the gym door. I tried backpacking near Yosemite in my 20s and suffered altitude sickness for hours. I've run a mile twice since I was in high school, and maybe three times before that. As soon as I start exercising I begin to feel things; the monsters within me wake up. I get mad and agitated and anxious.

I also don't like to be physically uncomfortable. I can't sleep on planes or in cars. I still can't vomit, and it takes a lot for me to cry.

I easily get headaches and strain muscles; I don't like the heat or the snow. I've never had physical grit.

I once thought my lack of grit was a character flaw; I now think it speaks to how uncomfortable I've been in my body my whole life. It takes a lot of energy to hold in Calls, to not cry or express rage. It's exhausting to act civilized when you're navigating the rim surrounding a giant black hole, when your anguish is invisible and probably of no interest to the world.

My safe place is the family room couch with a hot beverage, a fuzzy blanket, a great TV series, and my husband. Before Peter's email, I hung out there as often as possible, even when I started getting bored and sick of myself in that state of hiding. Watching episode after episode of the latest show, my safe haven turned into a trap, a shrunken life, with a deadly inner voice telling me all the reasons I shouldn't face the world, all the reasons I was bad for the world and the world was bad for me.

So the subject of Peter's email—AIDS Life/Cycle—scared the shit out of me. *To choose the Peter in me do I have to get on a bike?*

I knew his email would be something that demanded I make a choice. Life or death. Grow or die. My whole future was at stake. I don't know how I knew this, why it was this particular email that would begin to wake me up, but I knew it.

I sat at my kitchen counter when no one was around and finally opened it. I clicked on the AIDS/LifeCycle website which featured smiling faces of all kinds of people—young, old, fat, thin, athletic, many of them in costume, riding down the coast of California.

I looked at the pictures and thought of Peter. Something I didn't recognize began stirring in my body: a tingling mixture of terror and excitement. I wanted something new, and I realized I would have to work hard to get it. I didn't want to be Jim; I wanted to put as much distance between Jim and me as possible.

I had no idea who I would become if I did this ride, but I knew it would be someone I liked better than the person I was at the time. I was dying inside on that fence; like the Eagles sang in "Desperado,"

And freedom, oh freedom, well that's just some people talkin' / Your prison is walking through this world all alone.

I was scared I couldn't do it, that it would be one more thing I'd try and quit, but I had to go for it—and I didn't want to disappoint Peter, who'd raised the bar for me. He was a hero to me, and ultimately I wanted to become a hero to myself, to believe in myself and trust myself for the first time. I wanted to follow through.

My husband wasn't happy. He didn't think I had time to train to ride my bike 545 miles, and it wasn't practical because our kids were still in junior high. But I had to do it anyway, even if he didn't understand what was at stake for me. I had to be willing to upset him.

I bought a new white bike and named her Amelia Earhart, hoping she'd know how to keep flying and persevering long after I'd given up. I bought all the gadgets—an odometer, a bento box, two water bottle cages, fancy clip-in shoes with pedals to match. I bought cycling pants, shirts, gloves, and socks.

I had to raise $3,000, and I was scared to go public with that goal. Who was I to be doing the AIDS Ride? I had no direct connection with AIDS. Shouldn't I do something from my own suburban culture like the Avon Breast Cancer Walk instead? Wouldn't people understand that better? On the edge of that dark hole, I was afraid of being judged and ridiculed. But I still went for it.

I created a fundraising page and shared it online. For me it was "AIDS Ride or Die." I was that desperate to join inner Peter and distance myself from inner Jim.

Money and emotional support began pouring in. My email would notify me that someone had donated $50, $100, $500. Some people asked their friends who didn't know me to donate, and they did. Other AIDS cyclists donated to me. People lent me cycling clothes and texted me about feeling inspired and excited by my commitment. This support felt brand new and energizing!

My town is flat. To ride 545 miles along the coast of California would take some training on hills. A town called Orinda, an hour away, had a well-organized training group, and each Saturday morning I got up early and drove at dawn to train with a group of cyclists. It was scary. People knew each other, looked confident, had done it before. I was an outsider who didn't know anyone with AIDS.

People asked, *Why are you riding?* to connect with each other. Common answers included, *My brother died of AIDS when I was a kid* or *I'm HIV positive* or *I have friends who have lost people to AIDS.* I told people, *Someone I was close to committed suicide; in the same week I met an AIDS doctor, who sent me a link to The Ride.*

Very cool! they'd say, and they'd hug me.

As time went on, I got more comfortable sharing the part about how I'd been on the fence between life and death myself, and how I was finally ready to get off the fence and join life wholeheartedly. Many of the cyclists knew about life on the fence, too.

I created a playlist for my hour-long drive to Orinda. I meant for it to get me mentally prepared to push myself on my bike, to ride farther than I ever had before. What I didn't expect was for this playlist to became a set of anthems that would help me open my heart to life. Listening to the particular lyrics I had chosen took on new meanings as I packed, drove, rode, and recovered with consistency and commitment.

> *I'd catch a grenade for ya*
> *Throw my head on a blade for ya*
> *I'd jump in front of a train for ya*
> *You know I'd do anything for ya*
> *I would go through all this pain*
> *Take a bullet straight through my brain*
> *Yes I would die for you baby*
> *But you won't do the same*
> —"Grenade" by Bruno Mars

This song became entirely different for me than what Bruno Mars had probably meant. Instead of a *Boohoo I love you more than you love me, you screwed me over* song (my song for my first 46 years), I began to hear it as *I am working harder than I've ever worked for you* (the recipients of the millions of dollars raised by the AIDS Ride), *and it's irrelevant that I don't know you and that I won't receive the same effort from you. You deserve my effort because you're human and alive.*

This was the birth of my access to dignity! It was my first true experience of feeling unconditional love, of being willing to get deeply uncomfortable for others, even others I didn't know.

Each time I drove the hour to Orinda, I began to cry in the first five minutes and kept crying the whole way there. This surprised me each time. I'd pull out of my driveway and notice I felt nothing, then the music would start and so would the tears. Each song was support for dropping my self-protection and abandoning any score-keeping with life. For the first time, my cries weren't the result of sadness and broken-heartedness—they came from love.

> *Some are like water, some are like the heat*
> *Some are a melody and some are the beat*
> *Sooner or later they all will be gone*
> *Why don't they stay young?*
>
> *It's so hard to get old without a cause*
> *I don't want to perish like a fading horse*
> *Youth's like diamonds in the sun,*
> *And diamonds are forever*
> —"Forever Young" by Alphaville

I'm alive. I'm here. Life is short. What I do matters. I can help.

The last five to ten miles of every training ride was a nightmare for me. To distract myself, I'd count to 20 and count to 20 again. I'd look for milestones only 10 feet ahead of me: tree . . . bush . . . crack in the pavement . . . weed . . . piece of trash. Another crack in the road. I'd want nothing but to get off my damn bike. I wanted to throw a tantrum and quit. I stopped giving a shit about people with AIDS, or about anyone else for that matter. But I kept going because

I knew my relationship to life itself was at stake. As much as I wanted to quit, doing so would have been more painful than continuing. It would have been like a butterfly flipping off life and returning to the cramped old cocoon. I never quit.

One day closer to The Ride, we were peddling up Mount Diablo, 11 miles up without even a single flat stretch. I was suffering. Queen Mary, a grandmother and our glorious leader, stayed in the back of the pack with me. Just as I was about to lose it, she said, *Tell me about your kids.* That got me talking even as I gasped for air, and up we went around bend after bend. Mary'd had breast cancer and then a recurrence; she was in treatment then, but she rode anyway. She saw the preciousness of everyone, and she was the living bridge between our training group and successfully completing The Ride. With her help, cycling up Mount Diablo turned me into an athlete. *I'm an athlete!*

The Ride came. On Day 2—a full 107 miles from Santa Cruz to King City and our longest day—I suffered a knee injury and had to get on the support bus. It was decorated in a Flintstones and Jetsons theme, and disco filled the air, but the cheeriness didn't feel right—I had failed. Sitting alone on a seat near strangers who had various injuries or bike issues and who also had to call it a day, I complained out loud, *Today sucks.* The guy in front of me whipped around and said, *How do you know? What if this turns out to be the best day of your whole life?* He didn't say it in a bitchy way, but rather more like an angel trying to reach me. He was championing me to raise the bar on what was possible. *Good point*, I responded, and like a droopy plant that got some water, I perked up.

I made friends that day. On that bus we laughed, danced, sang songs, and told stories. We fell in love with each other. When we arrived early at the next campsite in King City, one of my new friends, Johnny, came up with the idea of setting up people's tents so that when they rode in, they'd have less work to do.

We walked to the giant trucks, grabbed tent after tent, and set them up in their designated places. Soon others joined us. Then, like little kids, we waited. *Who lives in that one? What are they gonna do when they see it?* Many arriving cyclists, exhausted and at the end of their ropes, cried when they saw what a bunch of strangers had done for them. As the guy on the bus had predicted, it was The Best Day Ever.

> *We who lived in the concentration camps can remember the men who walked through the huts comforting others, giving away their last piece of bread. They may have been few in number, but they offer sufficient proof that everything can be taken from a man but one thing—the last of the human freedoms—to choose one's attitude in any given set of circumstances, to choose one's own way.* (Viktor Frankl, *Man's Search for Meaning,* pp. 65–66)

Viktor highly valued the freedom we have to choose our attitudes: Peter's attitude of opening to life; my attitude of courage in choosing to ride; Queen Mary's attitude of kindness; the Bus Guy's attitude of encouragement; Johnny's attitude of generosity with the tents. All our attitudes are choices and in our control.

Attitude is more important than intelligence, success, or beauty. Attitude is our power in any moment. When we know this, we can change the world in an instant. We don't have to wait for the world to change for us.

Knowing we have the power to choose our attitude isn't simply something we tell ourselves. It's not "Fake it till you make it." It's authentic. It's a grounded choice from a permanent menu: Generosity, Appreciation, Gratitude, Courage. It doesn't mean you believe bad things are okay. It just means you're holding a paradox: even as the world is full of injustice and pain, we still have agency in what attitude we bring to the challenges.

I don't have to wait for sunshine, kind people, the weekend, physical health, a positive cash-flow, or a vacation to find generosity inside of me. I can find it in the rain, when my family is grumpy, when I have diarrhea or cancer, when I'm pulling money from dwindling savings, and when I'm overworking. I plan to find generosity on my deathbed when that time comes—because I can. And so can you.

Questions for Reflection:

1. Do you believe the universe is friendly or hostile? Why?
2. Do you have a Jim inside of you? A Peter? In other words, which parts of you want to die? Which parts of you want to live?
3. Think back to a meaningful moment in your life, a moment when you felt fully alive. What attitudes did you bring to that moment? Generosity? Love? Appreciation?
4. Did you know expectation is the fastest way to a bad mood? And appreciation is the quickest way to a good mood? Think of a current problem and find your expectation in it. Change your focus to appreciation for some aspects of the problem and see how your mindset changes for the better.

Actions to Immediately Increase Your Life Force:

1. Make a list of your heroes and at least five qualities you admire about each of them. These qualities are inside of you right now. Know this. Begin to think about how you can step into these qualities in your life *even more*.
2. Imagine you are going to train for a huge challenge like the AIDS Ride and create your playlist. Listen to it and let it inspire and strengthen you.

Chapter 5

CREATIVITY (VS. HOLDING BACK)

Creativity is saying *Yes* to some action, such as work or art.

According to Viktor Frankl, being creative—in work, or in the arts, or in deeds—is a primary source of meaning. Creativity allows us to transcend ourselves through action, to reach the world beyond us in a meaningful way. Doing our work, taking care of our families, engaging in artistic pursuits such as music, writing, and painting, showing kindness—even cooking and taking out the trash—are creative acts!

Each creative action requires a *Yes.* An authentic *Yes* stokes our life force.

In the movie *Yes Man,* Jim Carrey played a miserable guy named Carl who was stuck in a rut. Then he went to a self-help seminar and magic helped him unleash the power of *Yes.* He now had to say *Yes* to *everything.* And guess what? After things got a little messy, he fell in love, got a promotion, and transformed into a really happy guy.

Sometimes just one fearful *No* cuts us off from an explosion of opportunities.

Here's what I didn't understand for so long: life is continually saying *Yes* to us. Every single day we have sunrises and sunsets. Life grows plants and sustains animals and gives us so many things:

chocolate, sex, the Grand Canyon, stars, fire, the moon, and sea horses. Life offers us a feast. How much are you saying *Yes* back to life?

Yes, I'm going to jump in the ocean even though I flat-ironed my hair this morning. Yes, I'll try backpacking even though I'm scared of bears. Yes, I'll go out with that nice guy at work even though the last guy screwed me over. Yes, I'll buy the sad bank teller a coffee because it'll make her smile. Are you in touch with your heart-centered *Yeses*, the deep ones that transcend yourself and open doors to a more meaningful life?

Someone once said *Yes* to me in a way that astonished me. I had been working in a remote village in Ethiopia with my daughter Lauren who was then 17 years old. I tripped over some barbed wire, hit the ground hard with the weight of my whole body, and broke my hip. I couldn't walk, and there were no hospitals around, so right away I had to fly home for surgery. It was Easter Sunday, a busy day in Ethiopia, but the locals still helped me book my flights home.

When I woke up from surgery in California, a parade of nurses, hospital administrators, and doctors came to my room to thank me. *Huh? For what?*

Apparently, one of my clients had heard what had happened from a mutual friend. Since she was a surgical nurse at a busy hospital, she knew exactly what surgery teams love: good food. She created a beautiful antipasto plate with meats, cheeses, peppers, olives, and baskets of delicious breads; she even sent along three kinds of cookies. She wrote a card thanking the team for taking good care of me (which gave me the benefit of being cared for extra well!).

I was inspired. Not only was this an act of wild generosity, it was her *Yes* to providing a creative response to a problem. She made the situation so much better for all of us. I'll never forget it. How many times has a friend been ill or grieving and I've only offered a fraction of what this client did for me? I now know I can do better.

After surgery, when I was laid up in a hospital bed in my family room for weeks, friends did more to astonish and delight me. One brought six baby tomato plants and put them in my garden. Another read poetry to me. Others made food that was not only delicious but also looked like art: a roasted chicken on a platter surrounded by rings of colorful sides; a salad with pops of all the colors of the rainbow; a cake with frosting spread in swirls.

In graduate school I learned about Freud and his concepts of the id, the superego, and the ego. The id relates to the urges we feel from the animal part of us, such as wanting to have sex with the hot priest or wanting to shout at the checker in the grocery store for taking too long. The superego is the moral part of us that shames us for being so out of control, telling us that only bad people lust after hot priests or even consider being mean to innocent people in grocery stores. The ego runs interference between the two: *It's understandable that you find him attractive, but he's made a serious commitment to, so it's not really gonna happen. Breathe—that checker is doing the best she can with the groceries, and she's probably stressed out by the long line, too.*

The point is that we are taught to think of the id as the bad part of us, the part with no moral compass that wreaks havoc on the world, the part that acts on instincts like rabbits or squirrels do. But the id is actually the most spectacular part of all and deserves respect because the id is what fuels our lives with creativity and passion.

The id speaks to us through hints. How many times a day do you get an inkling to do something that might be risky or make you feel vulnerable but comes from your heart? These little inklings are the products of your inherent creativity. They come wrapped in a *Yes* before we get logical or cautious or practical and shut them down with a *No.* Learning to listen to these inklings opens the door to shifting any moment into a meaningful possibility.

When we want to bring the sad bank teller a coffee, it's the id that comes up with that idea. When my client first conceived of that Italian feast, the idea came from her id. When I told my future husband that I had a crush on him after two years of friendship, that was my id's idea. The id is the source of our creativity, of our passion for life. A human without an id is like a robot.

It's easiest to hear these inklings when we're feeling well, when we have energy and are in a good-enough mood. When we are sick or exhausted or lonely or trapped in a story, it's much harder because when we don't feel well, we contract in self-preservation. It's hard to think about the world *out there* when we've been captured by physical and emotional misery *in here.* When we are hunkered down, conserving our energy, inklings reach us more slowly, and sometimes they don't reach us at all.

When we are open to creative impulses, we work more effectively at our jobs. We have access to the deeper *Yes* in us to go the extra mile. I'm a significantly different therapist when I have energy and connection to my id than when I'm depleted. I am more attentive, loving, and creative on the spot. I'm listening for opportunities, ready to take chances to get out of the repetitive stories of the Default Network. I'm curious, inspired, and thinking on many levels at once.

The same goes for parenting. I don't know how tired your parent(s) were when you were growing up or how tired you are now if you're raising kids, but I know I was exhausted raising mine. In my unconscious pattern, I would conserve energy until I absolutely had to take action—I'd haul myself out of bed, quickly prepare something for breakfast, and order the kids to hurry up. This is how it was for early humans, who had to conserve their energy for hunting or dealing with harsh weather or fighting neighboring tribes. *Conserve, act when necessary; conserve, act when necessary. In short, survive.*

Survival mode and the id are not friends. Survival mode is so intense and hyper-focused that it misses the chance to hear the sweet songs of the id. On school mornings, my id might want to tell me, *Pause and look at the faces of your precious daughters. Take it in. Tell them something special you love about them.* I rarely heard the songs from my id when rushing my kids to school.

Raising my kids was most difficult when the holidays came around. So much was expected by the larger world when all I wanted to do was rest. My inner critic grabbed a megaphone and yelled at me more loudly than usual: *Why haven't you gotten pumpkins yet? Are you just gonna buy those crap costumes at the last minute again? Why can't you be like the other moms and make them yourself? Then the girls would feel REALLY loved.*

Every holiday and birthday provided extra reasons to feel bad about myself for falling short. I had to find a way to say *Yes* to celebration and fun and meaningful family rituals without a bad attitude. What did I genuinely have a *Yes* for on holidays? In survival mode I had no idea.

I developed my own rituals slowly, and I usually discovered them by chance. I saw a photo on Pinterest of a Gratitude Tree. It was so cheerful and festive that I made one for us before Thanksgiving. I walked out in nature and cut five large, whimsical branches to make the tree. I cut circles out of colorful paper, punched holes in them, and put them in a pile with a pen next to the branches. For days we wrote what we were grateful for in the circles and hung them on the tree. We've done this for years now, and we've made trees like this for friends. No matter what was going on in our family year after year, thankfulness was right there in the kitchen like a lighthouse.

One holiday season when our girls were young, I saw ceramic bowls filled with rocks and blooming paperwhite bulbs in a gift shop. They were so pretty that I wanted to grow some in my house. I found the bulbs in a hardware store and got pea gravel at a rock yard. Now I plant bulbs in November so that by Christmas they will be in full bloom and fragrant. I've done this every year since, even in the years when Christmas felt hostile and broken. Planting bulbs is like making a wish or a prayer for something beautiful to bloom.

I make wreaths for our front door. One year my id told me the Christmas wreath *had* to be made from eucalyptus leaves. Tom and I drove around the outskirts of our town with a saw, clippers, and a mini-ladder. We found a big old eucalyptus tree and cut a few branches. I loved its aroma and shimmery leaves, and I added red berries and cinnamon sticks for festivity. Walking up the path to my front door, even when I was dreading a conflict waiting inside, the wreath hung there reminding me of what trauma forgets—that the conflict was happening and festivity was, too. Not one, but both.

On the eve of our girls' birthdays, Tom and I blew up a bunch of balloons to cover their bedroom floor while they were sleeping. It was hard sometimes because we didn't always want to. Years into this ritual Tom would say, *Really? Again? Isn't 18 too old for this?* But the balloons were a colorful surprise that meant a lot to them. Even in their moody teenage years, they reminded us that they were expecting balloons.

I look back on these creative traditions as among my favorite moments with the kids. Even though I told you the bleak truth—that for years I was living on the fence between life and death—taking these creative actions were transcendent moments in which I could see and feel clearly: *I love Tom and our girls. I want to have hope for our family. I'm going to keep trying.*

I'm telling you about these creative achievements not to bore or impress you, but because they're actually miracles. *The orphan plants bulbs. The baby left alone in the crib makes a wreath. The four year old who stopped vomiting for good blows up balloons. The adolescent whose dad wouldn't look at her makes double animal pancakes.*

That's right—double animal pancakes. When our girls' friends slept over, I made double animal pancakes for breakfast. Each kid got to pick two animals, one for the head and one for the tail. Half horse and half spider; half penguin and half sloth; half gorilla and half shark. Even though these carefully poured shapes became messy blobs once the batter bled into itself, the kids looked at me with adoration. *Mom, this is SO GOOD! OMG Mom, I SEE it!*

Being creative can be a serious matter. Viktor and his friend saw a chance to escape the death camp and worked out the details. But as soon as they finalized their plans, Viktor felt gripped by an unpleasant feeling. As a doctor, he had been taking care of prisoners suffering from typhus. When he went to say goodbye to them and looked into their eyes, the bad feeling in him got worse. He realized that not abandoning them was more important to him than escaping; continuing to serve them was more meaningful than his own freedom.

> *Suddenly I decided to take fate into my own hands for once. I ran out of the hut and told my friend that I could not go with him. As soon as I had told him with finality that I had made up my mind to stay with my patients, the unhappy feeling left me.* (Viktor Frankl, *Man's Search for Meaning,* p. 58)

By definition, meaning is self-transcendent. Any action that transcends ourselves—from making double animal pancakes for kids to staying imprisoned to honor a commitment to others—makes us feel better, more connected, and more alive. In such cases we have used creativity to connect instead of holding back our most loving self. Misery, on the other hand, is rooted in too much "me" and disconnects us from others.

How can we, on a day-to-day basis, choose creating over withholding, serving over inaction? It's counterintuitive that Viktor or any of us would become more connected, peaceful, and joyful by forgoing our own immediate comfort—but we do.

A few years ago, I had a client named Phyllis who felt victimized by her stage IV cancer (which is reasonable, at first). She knew she was dying, and her teenage kids were staying away from her, probably because they were scared, and also because they were doing teenage things.

In her mind, life was treating her unfairly, and she believed she was getting the short end of every stick: her work colleagues didn't throw her the right retirement party, her doctor sucked, her ex-husband was a disappointment, and her friends said all the wrong things. She was (again reasonably) trapped in grievances centered on *me, me, me.*

She went to see Deepak Chopra for a weekend class, and he changed her life forever (and a bunch of other people's lives in the process). He told Phyllis, *Moment by moment, we choose miracle or grievance,* and she woke up to the possibility of miracles all around her. From that point on, she couldn't hide behind her grievances anymore.

When she'd start down a woe-is-me path, she'd interrupt herself. *Where's the miracle here? What can I say Yes to? Oh yeah, it's that my kids wanted to come visit me, finally!* Getting out of a victim mindset is the first step in shifting away from holding back and moving into creative action. Phyllis became an Olympian in non-victimhood in the last months of her life. She called herself out before anyone else could. She began noticing the miracles around her before anyone else did. *I had the nicest interaction at the doctor's office today!* she'd beam.

In my experience, dying people are the quickest to change in therapy. They have the most leverage working for them. Time is limited, so there is pressure and reason to change. Each day, each conversation, each decision counts. Their changes can be extraordinarily meaningful to their legacy, to everyone close to them at the end, and even to the people those people know.

During my last day visiting Phyllis at her house, she was too sick to see me, so I sat with her grieving brother, a big "manly" guy. I noticed a bottle of red nail polish on the kitchen table. After some time I said to him, *Want me to paint your nails?* He said, *Yes.* Later I learned that they put nail polish on Phyllis and on everyone in the family. And they all wore red nail polish to the funeral. The red nail polish became something fun and joyful, and to me it represented a miracle—the miracle of Phyllis and her ability to change an old mindset.

Perhaps the opposite of creativity is victimhood, blaming something outside us when things are not right, instead of creating something better. If you recall any time in your life that you've felt like a victim, you'll recognize there's a lack of creativity and a holding back of action. There's too much "me" in victimhood.

Phyllis found her way to the reality of everyday miracles before she died. Simply looking for miracles creates them. Grievances are a dime a dozen, and so are miracles if we remember to look for them.

When my hip broke, I was afraid of the surgery and of being unable to walk for weeks. I could have blocked out all the miracles, but they were there. The medical staff was kind; my client made a feast; the physical therapist who came to my house twice each week championed me back to walking; my community showed up with love. Miracles were everywhere. And they helped me with my own sense of creativity. As I sat there in the hospital bed recovering, I read a book that touched me, so I wrote a letter to the author thanking him for what he wrote, and he wrote back telling me how scared he was to write it. Miracles.

Meaningful creativity is authentic. It doesn't deplete us or make us hold our breath or sneak cigarettes in the backyard. When it's a happy occasion, saying *Yes* makes us feel bubbly and fulfilled inside. When it's a sad occasion—when we take the day off work to help a friend who lost her mom or cook a meal for a family in trouble—we may not feel bubbles, but we will feel peace.

That psychiatrist who rescued me three times when I was a baby may have felt a sense of danger and anguish, but he acted anyway. He said *Yes* to involving himself when he didn't have to. He may have done this with lots of people over the course of his career, and every time he did, I'd wager that he went to bed at night knowing he had leaned in and done what he could do.

At the very least, authentic *Yeses* give us bubbles and/or peace. These moments of bubbles and peace don't go away; they last forever.

I had a migraine for 19 days straight leading up to and during Camp Kesem last summer; the last six days of my migraine were during camp. Shouting, singing camp songs, zip-lining, and playing capture the flag were not great for my head!

Every morning at camp I woke up early with my head pounding, and I would sneak into the lobby with my pre-packed bag of remedies: Excedrin Migraine pills, an eye mask, a large Ziplock Bag for ice from the ice machine, ground coffee, a cone and coffee filter, and an electric kettle—all in hopes that I might reduce the pain so I could function that day. It was hell.

On the last day of camp the older kids were scheduled to take a hike to a waterfall. It was a hot day and walking four miles round trip didn't sound good to me given my headache, but doing minimal activity wasn't helping either. So, to punish my migraine, I said *Yes* to the hike. When we arrived at the stream, I saw that one at a time, kids were sitting on top of the falls and pushing themselves off, dropping 10 feet into an ice-cold pool below. Since I'm terrified of heights, I definitely wasn't going to do that, so I sat in the shade of trees nearby and watched everyone else play.

When it was almost time to return to camp, two leaders, Coco and Drummer Boi, asked if I was going to jump. *No way!* I told them. They leaned closer, and Coco fiercely looked me straight in the eyes. She said, *Who do you want to be when we're walking back to camp, Sunflower* (my camp name), *the person who jumped, or the person who didn't!?* She went directly to the heart of the matter, confronting me with my very best philosophy! She turned the tables on me, hitting me where it hurt! Because in theory I don't believe anymore in playing small, I had no choice but to change my mind and say *Yes*.

I asked Coco and Drummer Boi to keep an eye on me in case I had a heart attack when I plunged into the freezing water. Wanting to save face with everyone else, I walked casually to the top of the falls, wearing hiking pants and a t-shirt instead of a bathing suit. I sat on my butt and scooted out to the very edge like it was no big deal. With my heart pounding I leaned forward, making sure the three lifeguards below understood that I was coming down, and I forced myself to drop. The cold water was shocking—worse than I had imagined. I scrambled to the edge of the water, triumphant, and when I climbed out, I realized I had left something behind—my migraine! Saying Yes cured me. Bubbles AND peace!

My understanding of the power of *Yes* became far more vivid when I read Viktor's book. It was the following line that blew me away:

> *What was really needed was a fundamental change in our attitude toward life. . . . It did not really matter what we expected from life, but rather what life expected from us. We needed to stop asking about the meaning of life, and instead to think of ourselves as those who were being questioned by life.* (Viktor Frankl, *Man's Search for Meaning,* pp. 76–77)

What?! Could life itself actually be asking something of me?? Before reading Viktor, I had never thought of life being the recipient of my efforts. In my well-worn path as a victim, I was simply disappointed and enraged at the hand I'd been dealt by life. But imagining life as a real force that was asking something of me flipped my paradigm upside-down! What if, all this time, life was right there in all its abundance, and the task of my whole life was to find a way to answer with my full engagement? What if anything less was pure disrespect? This new paradigm made it impossible to engage in blaming and ended holding back for good. It ruined both for me. Sure, I still try to blame and hold back often enough, but now I know better than to stay there for too long. I fundamentally don't believe in blaming and holding back anymore.

My answer to life had to be a wholehearted *Yes.* Nothing less, no matter what happened next.

Questions for Reflection:

1. What do you want to create? What work do you ultimately want to do? What kind of family culture do you dream of? How do you want to serve the world?
2. What gets in the way of your authentic *Yeses*? What is the cost to you when you block an authentic *Yes* by holding back?
3. What would happen if you stayed the course of your dreams more directly than you are now? What could help you? Who are your dreams' allies?
4. Which *Noes* in you come from fear? What would your life look like if you said *Yes* to one of them this week? How would you feel?

Actions to Immediately Increase Your Life Force:

1. Do something right now that you have an authentic *Yes* for but have been avoiding, such as signing up for a 5K or inviting a friend to do something fun or writing a letter to connect or making an overdue apology or buying that camera lens you've been wanting but haven't felt entitled to. Notice how your physiology immediately changes when you take action on an authentic *Yes* instead of shutting yourself down with an inauthentic, fear-based *No*. Enjoy the shift! With more energy, begin to think of what you might do next!
2. Think of someone or something you're blaming in your life right now. Imagine your blame is a clue to a hidden creative action you are avoiding taking. What could it be? Get curious! See how shifting your attention from blame to curiosity about creative action affects your physiology and mood.

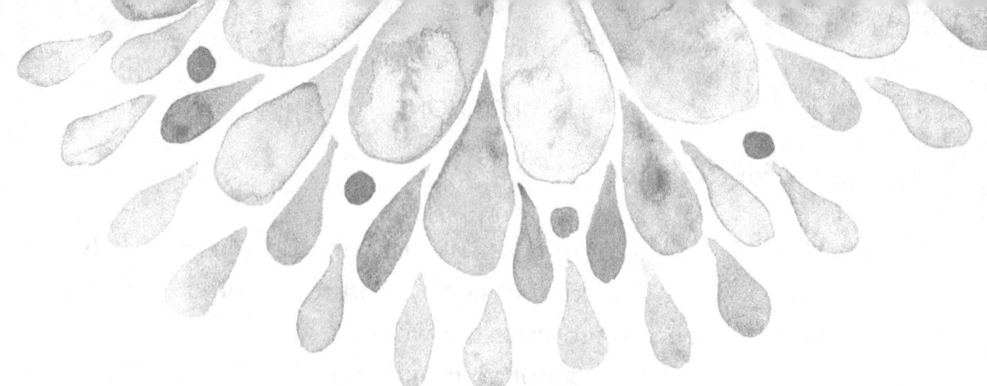

Chapter 6

HEALTHY SUFFERING
(VS. MISGUIDED SUFFERING)

> *When a man finds that it is his destiny to suffer, he will have to accept his suffering as his task; his single and unique task. He will have to acknowledge the fact that even in suffering he is unique and alone in the universe. No one can relieve him of his suffering or suffer in his place. His unique opportunity lies in the way in which he bears his burden.* (Viktor Frankl, *Man's Search for Meaning*, pp. 77–78)

Viktor talks about suffering in a fresh way that turns our cultural bias against suffering on its head. He helped me make friends with suffering and convinced me that suffering is actually meaningful and a necessary part of being human.

We admire stories about everyday heroes who go through the unimaginable—the loss of a child or soul mate, a brutal rape, quadriplegia, cancer, a school shooting—and who suffer with courage and grace. We all know physical and emotional suffering is coming someday, and we all dread it. People who show us how to deal with suffering help us believe that we, too, can do so when we must.

In American culture, where we have only three days to grieve before getting back to work, it is impossible to keep a job and grieve fully. So the culture unwittingly pressures people to move out of their grief quickly; but we don't move out of it quickly. We may act like we do, but we don't, not when our loss has so radically changed our lives and our identities and our futures.

Many years ago, a dear Jewish friend lost an immediate family member. She is still grieving. At the time I learned about the Jewish mourning practice called "sitting shiva," during which friends and extended family members visit the grieving immediate family for seven days to offer comfort.

For many months following my friend's loss, a large support circle of her friends provided meals, errands, child-care, and loving gifts. I watched my friend receive more support than I'd ever seen following a death. It was beautiful. To me, it seemed like a miracle. I am ashamed to say I was envious—my birth mother and my adoptive parents had never shown me love like this love.

With every dinner delivered, trip to the grocery store taken, help with house cleaning and childcare my friend received, I felt more and more envious. My envy started to feel like my overwhelming childhood anger. After all, I, too, have felt grief stricken over the loss of my biological family, but few people believe adoption is anything to grieve. *Why not me?! I need support too! I lost a mom, a dad, six sisters, four grandparents, 14 aunts and uncles, and scores of cousins! Where is my Helping Hands website? Where is my shiva? Where is my nurturing community?*

My envy was getting in the way of my open heart, so I carefully confessed it to my friend. She is the kind of person who loves me no matter what. She understood, and she actually cried for me, and I cried for her. She knew that by my telling her about my envy, my heart was opening to her, not turning against her.

I hadn't realized I had lost a single thing until I was in college. I had really just thought I was bad and responsible for my lot in life. I found out the truth by surprise.

Until college I was too ashamed to date anyone. My dad's rejection made me fear that every guy would reject me, too. Then I met someone in my freshman dorm, and we fell in love. Every new experience of being seen and touched overwhelmed me with the terror of impending rejection. In my mind I was still that giant, red-headed, five-year-old monster who lumbered along, towering over my friends. I believed the closer this guy got to me, the quicker he'd see that I was a rotten egg and abandon me. But he didn't, and I started to feel like a real human being.

In our relationship, I quickly became unrecognizable to myself. Being right next to him in the nest of his dorm room was the safest feeling I'd ever had, and leaving his side for a class or an errand felt nearly unbearable. My schoolwork, my job, and my friends faded far into the background. He became my universe, and after just one quarter I was put on academic probation because I only passed one class. Looking back, it was like I had returned to infancy, the baby finally with her parent, safe and loved.

During our first summer apart, we wrote each other "orphan letters"—his parents had left him when he was a baby, too. Our love sounded like, *Without you, I feel like the last living animal on earth.* I felt panicked being away from him, and I kept track of the days and hours until I'd see him again: *56 days, 10 hours; 44 days, 23 hours; 32 days, 16 hours.*

I make jokes about this now, but I truly thought I would die when he broke up with me at 6:45 a.m. on Sunday, April 28, 1985. I remember the day as if a death had occurred. I had been thrown out of the love nest, and in an instant all the color drained from my life.

I still didn't cry; I didn't know how yet. Instead, in three months I gained 30 pounds, drank a lot of alcohol, started using cocaine, and withdrew from college for two quarters. I was spiraling out of control, and I needed to see a therapist. My mom paid for as much therapy as I needed for the next 11 years.

My new therapist asked me what was happening in my body. *Where do you feel it? Does it have a shape, a texture, a color?* I answered,

I have no idea and I just want to talk about my boyfriend who dumped me and how to get him back.

My therapist patiently and skillfully suggested over time that my pain was deeper than I realized, that it went all the way back to the beginning of my life. *What was she talking about? My adoption no longer affected me. My problems were here and now. I'd lost the love of my life, my only shot at happiness. My future was doomed. I was monstrously fat; my true ugliness was now impossible to disguise. No one would ever love me again.*

She told me I wasn't responding to a breakup in a normal 20-year-old way. Hmm. That made me curious.

Months later I was shopping in a record store in Berkeley, and a song started playing overhead. I didn't know the band and hadn't heard the lyrics before, but I broke down sobbing for the first time in my post-infant life. It wasn't the sobbing of a 20 year old, it was primal, animal sobbing. I didn't know what was happening, and I thought I was dying.

Once I stopped crying, I became obsessed with finding that song. I knew it mattered, but I didn't know why.

After paying about a hundred dollars on the wrong records, I found Eric Clapton's "Bell Bottom Blues" on a Derek and the Dominos album.

Bell bottom blues, you made me cry.
I don't want to lose this feeling.
And if I could choose a place to die
It would be in your arms.

Do you want to see me crawl across the floor to you?
Do you want to hear me beg you to take me back?
I'd gladly do it because
I don't want to fade away.

I wasn't singing to my boyfriend anymore, but realized at last that I was singing to my first mother. My therapist had been right all along.

I entered two years of intense emotional crisis. My tears were finally ready to flow for the first time since I was a baby, and I was terribly frightened. I cried in waves and feared that the intensity of my crying would kill me.

Each morning the crying started as a sickening feeling in the pit of my stomach. It rose up into my chest and throat with overwhelming force. I'd leave the classroom and go to the student health center, already crying when I arrived. They got to know me there and offered me a bed in a private room. At the same time, I worked part-time at a fancy restaurant. As I was taking an order at a table, I would feel the crying coming up in my chest, and I'd go inside the walk-in freezer to let some of it out like the foreshocks of an earthquake.

The waves of crying didn't feel relieving; they were scary as hell, especially at night. There were times when I cried so hard I felt like my organs were wringing themselves out before filling right back up again. Sometimes I thought I would literally die from desperate sadness. I wondered, *Is this what I felt as a baby? Are these baby-body memories that are finally coming out? Are memories stored as physical, cellular entities that persist for years?*

My therapist told me to trust the process, to trust my body. *It will cry as long as it needs to,* she said, *and then the crying will subside.* I didn't believe her. I thought I was a special case. I imagined getting locked up in a psych ward for life. But miraculously, two years later, it did stop. Like the gradual end of the flu, it dissipated.

A few years later, when I was 28, I went camping in Death Valley, a beautiful desert with pink and purple mountains. Seemingly out of nowhere, I had a late-night vision of a beautiful house with organic gardens, a chef, yoga classes, massages, and group therapy. I envisioned an integrative cancer center, a place where very sick and dying people would gather to find support and create community. I cried again.

In that moment I knew I wanted to work with cancer patients, even though I'd never interacted with one. I could relate to the scary place where both life and death are right there as options, co-existing in an immediate way. I could support cancer patients to believe their life held value no matter how diminished they felt, but what I couldn't have anticipated was how much cancer patients would also help me to find a sense of meaning in my own life.

> *A sense of meaning cannot be expected to spontaneously arise on its own, but instead each of us is vested with the responsibility of searching for meaning and finding those responsibilities, experiences, and roles in life for which we are each irreplaceable. Each of us must confront what life is demanding of us at each moment and must choose how we respond to what life gives us, both joyful and challenging. Meaning, in fact, is created moment to moment.* (William Breitbart, MD, *Meaning-Centered Group Psychotherapy for Patients with Advanced Cancer,* p. 8)

When I got home from the desert, I researched local cancer organizations and found one I wanted to work for. I walked right in and met with Karen, a cancer survivor and the director. On the spot, she hired me as a psychology intern, and I was about to embark on a journey that would open doors to experiencing human suffering and wonder.

The Cancer Support and Education Center, a nonprofit associated with Stanford University Medical Center, offered a uniquely deep, creative, and integrative approach to cancer. For the most part, this wasn't a program for people who had been diagnosed, gone through treatment, and gotten back to their lives. This was a program for people who had recurrences and a poor prognosis, who were likely going to die and knew it.

Once a week, for 10 weeks, clients and their support person would come to an all-day group of about 20 people. Our interdisciplinary team—including nutritionists, body workers, imagery facilitators, art therapists, dance therapists, and meditation teachers—had the goal of helping clients heal physically, if possible; if that was not possible, we helped them heal psychologically and spiritually. The goal was for clients to come to a place of freedom and peace no matter their physical outcome.

I witnessed emotional and spiritual healing happen for many people. We planned and experienced our deaths. We examined which parts of us wanted to die and which wanted to live. We looked at secondary gains of cancer—how cancer allowed people to leave jobs and marriages they didn't want, how cancer allowed people to repeatedly say *No* for the first time—and also say *Yes!* How could patients learn to support these secondary gains with or without the cancer?

In the program we used the whole group for healing:

> *Mary, how are you today?*
> *Well, I feel like 100 pounds is sitting on my shoulders.*
> *Joe! Be the 100 pounds! Press down on her shoulders. Mary, is that okay?*
> *Yes.*
> *How are you now?*
> *I've got this voice telling me I'm not doing enough. Not trying hard enough.*
> *Where do you hear it relative to your head?*
> *It's here on the left.*
> *Catherine! Stand on the left and tell her she's not doing enough. Not trying hard enough.*
> (Tears start.)
> *What's happening?*
> *I'm just so mad.*
> *What does mad have to say?*
> *Well, I'm not supposed to be mad.*

> *Alaina! Stand near Mary and tell her she's not supposed to be mad. Mary, what are you mad about? If mad had a voice, what would it say?*
>
> *I'm tired of this! I don't want to get chemo anymore! I'm not even doing it for myself at this point. I'm doing it for everyone else. I'm ready to rest. I want peace.*

More tears came, and a look of relief that she'd spoken her truth came over her face. Her husband held her and cried with her. They realized they needed to reconsider her aggressive treatment. Was it time to stop? It was. With the support of the group, she had found the truth.

Once true expressions of suffering are allowed in a community, it is easier for all involved to relax. When the depths of pain are witnessed and supported, the lighter stuff starts to happen; laughter and play become possible, too.

Fred, an adult choir director with stage IV colon cancer, and his partner were in my first group. Fred told us he had called his mom in New York. *How are you?* she asked. *Not too good,* he replied. *I'm shitting blood, and the chemo is exhausting me; I'm in pain all the time, and the cancer has spread to my liver and bones. Well, besides all that, how are you?* she asked. We all burst into laughter, and he told us he wanted to sing "Zippity Doo Dah" for his check in, in honor of his mother. We sang, howling with laughter.

When Fred was dying a few months later at his home in San Francisco, his choir secretly practiced "Somewhere Over the Rainbow" and sang it to him from the driveway outside his bedroom window. We heard that Fred, though he could no longer speak, smiled.

Years later, when I was raising my young kids and had my own private practice, people with cancer often asked if I'd start a group. Not only did I not have time, I wondered how could I make a group nearly as valuable as those at the Cancer Support and Education Center.

In 2008, I discovered a clinical trial at Memorial Sloan-Kettering Cancer Center in New York. Under Dr. William Breitbart's leadership, psychiatrists there were trying to address the problem of despair in advanced cancer patients. Despair isn't like depression; despair is a spiritual problem stemming from a lack of meaning and a loss of hope for the future. An anti-depressant won't help.

At MSKCC they applied Viktor Frankl's work to late-stage cancer patients who were stuck in despair. In an eight-week "meaning-centered psychotherapy group," advanced cancer patients were helped in a systematic way to connect with a sense of meaning, peace, and purpose even as they approached the end of life.

In the trial, patients were assigned to either a meaning-centered group or a traditional cancer support group that tends to deal with more practical issues, such as coping with symptoms and exploring treatment options.

Patients were assessed before and after completing the eight-week program and again two months later. They measured spiritual well-being, hopelessness, desire for death, optimism, pessimism, anxiety, depression, and overall quality of life.

The outcomes of the trial were significant for patients in the meaning group.

After just eight weeks, patients reported improved quality of life and sense of meaning as well as decreased anxiety, hopelessness and desire for a hastened death!

What excites me even more is two months later, patients in the meaning group reported even *more* improvements, but there was no significant improvement on any of the variables for patients in the traditional support group.

I wrote to Dr. William Breitbart expressing interest in exactly what they did in the eight-week program, and he generously sent me detailed materials.

In early 2009 I gathered four people with various serious illnesses in my hometown to form a pilot group that followed Dr. Breitbart's protocol. Two had cancer and two had debilitating metabolic diseases. After eight weeks together, the participants found the experience extremely valuable. But we didn't feel finished, so we added more people. Eleven years later, this group still meets Mondays at noon for 90 minutes of cultivating meaning. We lost one of our original four members to breast cancer, but the other three original members are still in the group. We like to say our mission is cultivating meaning and defying individualism in the face of tragedy.

What exactly is *Meaning*?

In numerous workshops I have asked this question to a wide variety of people: the young and the old, the sick and the healthy, the joyful and the despairing. I've asked this question of therapists from all over the world, too. Even though we all recognize meaning because we are human, defining it is difficult.

People say, *My work has meaning because I help a lot of people. The love I feel for my family has meaning. Being near the ocean has meaning. The story of my grandparents escaping the war has meaning. Supporting reforestation to protect the future of the earth has meaning. The attitude of generosity in the face of suffering has meaning.* Everyone easily understands these things have meaning because we are human.

Here are a couple of questions that are easier to answer: How do you know when something has meaning for you? How does meaning feel in your body?

Everyone I've worked with seems to agree that in the body, meaning feels present, clear, loving, joyful, warm, connected, expansive, light, open, generous, aware, safe, coherent, flowing, peaceful, and calm.

Meaning is so big, it lives in the body, mind, and spirit all at once. It's too big to compartmentalize.

Viktor believed that meaning is our primary motivation in life.

I once asked Claude how he defined meaning, and right off the bat he said this:

Meaning seems to connect our embodied self with a larger, universal experience, so that what we do to satisfy ourselves seems to also satisfy the universe. That's the best definition of meaning I've ever heard.

Viktor identified three sources of meaning:

1. Work/creativity
2. Experiences
3. Our attitude in the face of inevitable suffering

But with the help of Viktor's teachings, I see six sources of meaning:

1. Experiences—connecting with life (love, beauty, humor)
2. Creativity—actively engaging in life (roles, work, deeds, accomplishments)
3. Love—who, what, where we love
4. History—defining stories and memories
5. Life as a Living Legacy
6. Attitudes—encountering life's inevitable limitations

After seeing with my own eyes how well people with life-altering tragedies respond to Viktor's work, I had to wonder: must one experience a certain amount of serious, life-and-death kind of trauma to truly understand and benefit from Viktor's work? Put another way, can people who have received only "bumps and bruises" in life benefit from traditional psychotherapy, whereas those of us with "missing limbs" and lost loves *must have* meaning-centered therapy to heal?

One of the main questions my clients ask in one form or another is, *I don't want to be here anymore, and I don't know how to feel differently about it, so why should I stay here, alive on this planet? Why isn't an expedited death better?* This is a question I understand because I, too, asked it for decades. Part of the problem is feeling so misunderstood by the world.

Many Jews died very soon after their release from the concentration camps; Viktor compared them to deep-sea divers coming up to the surface too fast. Non-prisoners simply didn't understand what the camps had been like; what the prisoners had lived through and lost; how much they truly had suffered. Viktor said non-prisoners would say, *I understand; I've suffered too in my life.* The lack of genuine understanding reflected in these comments drove a wedge between the prisoners who were trying to recover from severe trauma and a world that didn't understand them.

I hear this kind of thing all the time as an adoptee. *My parents divorced when I was little, and I never met my dad, so I know what it's like.* Or, *I grew up with abusive parents, and I always wished I was adopted.* These comments used to really upset me because they failed to acknowledge my core pain: *I grew up entirely disconnected from my whole lineage, and I had no say in it or explanation for it. I was purchased by a couple who were infertile, and it was my job to fulfill their dream of being parents. I'd have given anything to belong to someone in my real family instead of choking in the shame of being given away by them.* Ignorant comments are like telling an amputee that you understand because you sprained your leg once or had knee surgery.

When others don't, can't, or blatantly won't see our suffering, it's hard to feel secure and be reconciled to our lives. Adoptees have a four times greater suicide rate, even when they are adopted at birth. The culture is only beginning to understand the ways many current practices of adoption cause harm and why many countries prohibit it. Being culturally misunderstood is a factor in suicide.

I have learned how to respond to clients who finally say they want to die by suicide. They need to be deeply understood. Their pain needs to be uncovered and related to. I say, *Suicide is definitely an option. But it's one that requires careful consideration. It's a decision that should be made with the greatest care and only after all other options are exhausted. Why don't we make an agreement to put off the option of suicide for six months and work like hell together to see if we can find some reasons that make sense for you to stay here, to stay alive here on planet Earth. Then in six months we will re-evaluate. What do you think?*

Everyone says *Yes*. Everyone. Knock on wood, no one I've worked with has ever died by suicide. But many, many clients have wanted to or had tried earlier in their lives to kill themselves. Being able to talk about it without being shamed or prematurely forced into the hospital opens a door to a possibility that there is another way. The suicidal part is symbolic for the yearnings that need care. These deeper Calls just want to be seen and understood. They want to be valued, loved, and integrated.

There are alternatives to the dismal story that life isn't fair, that you are doomed, that it's all hopeless. Let's go find that bridge, not to jump off but to walk across together. Let's take a couple of steps past the tangled undergrowth to see if we can get a glimpse of the land of meaning beyond. That land is waiting for you; it always has been. But I won't tell you this so directly. Instead, we will step toward it together until you begin to see it for yourself. As you feel understood in the deeper places, your senses will begin to risk opening up again; you'll start to describe meaningful aspects of life that have been there all along, submerged beneath despair. When those six months have passed, the weather will have improved, the view will be wider, and we will need to raise our voices above the music to hear each other speak.

Connecting to meaning is the only way out of despair. I wouldn't know this or anything about helping others stay alive if I hadn't had to figure out how to do it for myself. Meaning is the key.

When a client loses her beloved husband and asks, *What should I do? How do I make this pain pass more quickly?*

I say, *The only thing to do for now is to endure each day. Let the waves of grief overtake you. They'll get smaller over time. You just endure.*

How long? she asks.

I tell her, *This will continue for a long time, but after six months it will start to get a bit easier. There will still be big waves of grief, but they will come a little further apart. For now, just endure. Devote yourself to experiencing your grief. Each time you cry it's productive and honest. Stay the course; it's the most efficient way.*

Grieving can have its traps. If we consider the loss, the thing that must be grieved, as a "first dart to the heart," the "second dart"—what we tell ourselves about the loss—can be a harmful trap. *You didn't do enough for your husband. You're always gonna be alone. You're gonna end up homeless because you understand nothing about finances.* These "second darts" are alarming, shameful, made-up problems that arise from our judging minds, originating from our Default Network. These thoughts need to be identified and extinguished as they are never helpful. We can learn with practice to tell these second darts to be quiet.

The Russian philosopher Fyodor Dostoevsky said, *There is only one thing that I dread: not to be worthy of my sufferings.*

How do we become worthy of our sufferings? We suffer as long as we need to because doing so is honest, and we do our best not to get distracted by "second darts." When we are ready, we transcend our circumstances by turning our suffering into meaning. We use our suffering to connect to others and serve the world—that's when we start to feel like our lives make sense again.

Suffering has offered me opportunities I could never have had without it. I wouldn't want to go through my life again or wish my life on someone else, but I appreciate having a hard-earned sense of belonging to the world. I like that I can help shattered people. I am so appreciative of Tom and our daughters, and that we stayed together against the odds. I am a person who is easily pleased, not because I'm a simpleton, but because I know what destitution feels like. I know the deadly kind of loneliness. Only through suffering could I have found a friendly universe, and love.

Questions for Reflection:

1. What are your deep beliefs about suffering? Do you think suffering is a normal part of life? Or do you think it's unnecessary—something only weak people experience?
2. How have you suffered in your life? How exactly did you relate to your suffering? Did you give it time, a voice, a community? Did you ignore it, cover it with addictions, move on as quickly as possible?
3. These days, does suffering open you or close you?
4. How have your heroes approached their suffering? Is their response to their suffering related to why they are your heroes?

Actions to Immediately Increase Your Life Force:

1. Write your answers to the six sources of meaning. Knowing what's meaningful to you allows you to consciously make choices that both nourish your soul and buffer you during the inevitable stresses in life.

    - What experiences—what sounds, sights, colors, tastes, smells, textures do you enjoy most (i.e., snow, trees, classic rock, avocado toast, coffee, corduroy, bare feet in the sand)?
    - What actions, causes, or jobs are meaningful to you (i.e., working, volunteering, playing music, writing, cooking, playing sports, gardening)?
    - Which people, places, and times (i.e., autumn, sunrise, Thanksgiving) do you love?
    - What stories—yours or others'—are most special to you?
    - In what ways do you want to create a legacy for the future (i.e., protecting the environment, supporting a

social justice issue, raising a child, being kind to strangers to cause ripples of kindness in the world)?
- Which attitudes do you most value when you or others suffer (i.e, courage, kindness, generosity, open-heartedness, compassion, integrity, commitment, appreciation, humor)?

2. From your worst experiences of suffering, what opportunities for growth and connection have arisen? Hold awareness of both the pain and the opportunity at the same time: *my cancer and my new friendship with Patty; my divorce and my commitment to the 5K; the death of my mother and a feeling of confidence that I did right by her.*

Chapter 7

RESPONSIBILITY (VS. ANARCHY)

If you were a better underachiever than I was, then you didn't graduate from high school because I came as close to not graduating as a person can. My senior award was "Most Absences & Still Graduated."

It wasn't that I was bored in class and needed more stimulation, the way some underachievers are. With the *fucks* on the bricks, my anger had already broken through any "good girl" facade I might have worn, and I simply had a *No* for any expectations directed at me from my mom and school. I didn't agree to the terms of the life I was living. I had never signed any contract to be the legal daughter of my parents, and I hated being stuck with them, so why should I play by society's rules?

Conforming would have felt like suffocating, like giving up, so with passion and sometimes glee I became an underachiever, and I think that saved me—the real me.

I wonder if every underachiever is expressing a vital, symbolic message—that in some way, there is too much unfairness, too little authenticity, and a crucial disconnect between the outside world and the inside truth. Even though our body might still be sitting in the classroom chair, we have walked away from the game.

Underachievement was how I told the truth—that I wasn't okay, that I didn't agree to decisions made by others about my life, that I was still in there, alive—because a rebel is fighting for *something.* It's when a rebel gives up and stops fighting that they are in real danger.

I later learned that rebellious kids have an easier time healing from their childhood issues because they've already said *No* to at least parts of the system—to their family system, to their religion, to their learning environment. Compliant kids act like they agree with all aspects of the system because they've never expressed a real no; they may not even know that they have a no!

As a young adult it encouraged me to think I might have a leg up on all the seemingly well-adjusted kids. It's easy to feel a lot of shame as an underachiever because adults are disappointed in you and other kids might think you're fun, but they don't necessarily respect you.

My mom was the quintessential good girl. President of her class, an undergrad at UC Berkeley, and a graduate student at Stanford, she was conscientious and dependable. She taught English at my high school and woke up at 3 a.m. to make her lesson plans and grade papers. She even won teaching awards. On top of that, she didn't swear, and she hired Nordstrom to dye her shoes to match her outfits. She was so proper and compliant that my underachievement by comparison was flagrant and outrageous. The contrast was agonizing, so to bring her down a few notches to my level, I tried to shock her and mess with her.

During lunch in high school I went home and drank my parents' whiskey. I watched soap operas and wrote notes to the office saying I'd had brain surgery and wouldn't return to school for a couple of weeks. My mom brought the notes home, horrified and embarrassed, but what could she do? I'd say, *You're not my real mom. Find my real mom and I'll listen to her!* I was in charge of me now. My mom had no leverage.

But I did want to go to college—not for college, but to get out of my parents' house. So I played both sides—I did enough work to get good grades while I skipped school as much as possible. I also benefitted from the help of teachers who were my mom's friends. Mr.

Cross, my history teacher, told me with a wink that I could skip the whole semester, and the lowest grade he'd give me was a B. So I did.

The downside of underachievement was I had no sense of self-respect. I treated my body like a trashcan and lived on sugar, sugar, and more sugar. I'd eat a dozen doughnuts or a whole batch of cookie dough or a box of Lucky Charms, trying to sweeten my life and comfort myself. I had nothing to offer the world and the world had nothing to offer me. I was stuck.

But I had always loved to sing. Our town's high school had an elite Madrigals group, and Mr. Lindsey was the colorful and perfectionistic choir director. He drove a powder-blue convertible, the chrome always shiny; he was intensely respected, but also feared. You didn't want to get on his bad side.

When I was in eighth grade, he painted the inside of my parents' house during the summer. He was a perfect painter. I was intimidated by him, but I hung around him at the house because my dream was to be in Madrigals. They had special costumes and traveled to Europe and Japan. Madrigals was the coolest thing.

When he finished painting that summer, he told me, *Pam, I've talked to your choir teacher, and she tells me you can sing. You just keep doing your best in choir, and one day you'll be a Madrigal.* I didn't know if he meant it, but I sure hoped he did.

That dream was the one thing that stayed important to me as I entered high school. When I started skipping classes, I still went to choir. I was still devoted to Mr. Lindsey's opinion of me and to my Madrigal future. But junior year I screwed even that up. I started skipping his classes, too. Once I was home cutting morning classes, I couldn't rally myself to get back onto campus for choir after lunch. I just couldn't.

So when it came time to try out for Madrigals, I didn't do that either. I figured I had already eliminated myself as a Madrigal; why did I need Mr. Lindsey to reject me, too? I wasn't a masochist. Well,

I kind of was, but not enough to want to see my name missing from the posted list of new Madrigal singers.

The next year, my senior year, I saw my classmates in Madrigals in their velvet green and maroon costumes at school preparing for performances. I heard about their outings on the loudspeaker during announcements. I couldn't even look at them. They were people who had stayed the course. They were good and normal. They reminded me how broken and bad I was.

That year I had four classes, the minimum we were allowed to take, but four were too many for me.

Madame Oliva was my mean French teacher. Like Agatha Hannigan in *Annie,* she bullied and humiliated students. I was drawn to her nastiness, and I wanted to bully her back. The way she treated students gave me a chance to get some of the rage out of my body. Without Madrigals, I had nothing left to lose.

In her class I repeatedly raised my hand and asked her why she was so mean. Did she realize how she made people feel? Did she feel good about herself at night? I had so much pent up rage, targeting her was a compulsion. I couldn't help myself.

I later learned from Jim that when we have a cannon inside of us that fires shots at people, it always swivels both ways—outside *and* inside. We can't be mean to the outside without also being mean to the inside. It's true—I was just as mean to myself as I was to Madame Oliva. And I'm sure she was as mean to herself as she was to students.

Madame Oliva called a meeting with the principal, the vice principal, the department head, and my mother. She said, *Pam ruins my day every day. I want her removed from my class.* The principal said, *Done.* I happily left; now I only had three classes.

When I got my high school yearbook at graduation, I saw the Madrigals sprinkled throughout the photos—Madrigals this and Madrigals that. It was the last thing I had really cared about, and I had ruined my chance. Looking back, I couldn't have done anything differently. I didn't have the confidence, the sense of my right to belong, or the capacity for hard work in me . . . yet.

Underachievement is not really freedom. It just looks and feels like freedom sometimes, like being free from going to class or work or getting dressed for the day; like being free to binge watch Netflix or blow off going to the dentist. But underachieving is not freedom. It's living half-dead, trapped in self-protection. It's giving up on the world and staying small. It's an act of rage or a passive suicide, or both.

Like bulimia or alcoholism, underachievement is something a person needs to recover from. The survival brain says, *Binge and purge! Drink more! Don't care!* To recover from underachievement means a person has to find something to care about and learn to hang in there with caring, even though the inner voice screams, *I'll be a sellout if I start to care! I'll die if I start to care!*

Going from a state of underachievement to a state of caring feels as big as going from one planet to another—New York City to the desert, winter to spring, caterpillar to butterfly, addicted to sober.

There's a pivot point, a threshold between the worlds.

Sometimes the pivot point happens in a moment, such as when a person gets a DUI or loses a friend or hits rock bottom. Other times the threshold takes years to cross. I was an adult now, and I was tired of not caring. But I didn't know what to care about, and my survival brain only knew that caring meant danger.

I couldn't relate to the idea of working in an office or playing Bunco with a group of women or volunteering at a school—I'd just feel invisible in the seeing "normalcy" of it all and start rebelling again.

To learn to care, I needed to start with something I could relate to—and after my desert vision of an integrative cancer center, I realized it was death that gave me a shot at caring. I had to start with death. Nothing else would work.

Trying to care was what brought me to my internship at the Cancer Support and Education Center. The heart of the program was a 10-week group, and I was required to fully participate in one session even though I didn't have cancer.

I was afraid of being seen by the participants as an outsider, an interloper, but their focus was on needing help, not on me. They were battling something that was threatening their lives. Cancer hurt them, controlled them, minimized them, exhausted them, made them feel ugly and angry. I didn't know exactly what it was like to be in their shoes, but as I listened, my life didn't feel so different. I was battling death, too, and in a way, I always had been. So I wasn't shocked or scared by their pain; I felt warmth in my heart for them. I leaned into my work with them. I became *for* them.

A compassion woke up in me—for them and for myself. I discovered that I had a deep interest in their physical suffering. I wanted to help them ease their nausea, the pain in their bones, their fatigue.

As an adult, I now know that physical pain was with me from the beginning of my life. Newborns get fed every three hours or so; being alone for hours in that apartment and hungry as an infant must have physically hurt. When my first mom hit and shook me, that must have hurt.

Working with physical pain in cancer patients was an entry point—a portal—for me to connect with the larger world. I naturally and easily care about people's physical pain. Over the years, clients have been surprised by this. They apologize for talking about symptoms plaguing them, worrying I'm bored or annoyed, but I consistently find I have infinite patience for their complaints.

I put physical pain in the center of our session because pain is very difficult to ignore or talk over. When someone is nauseous, I want to help them with just that. Nausea is enough. Trying to talk about issues and maintain social awareness when you have nausea makes nausea worse! Focusing on one thing at a time calms a stressed, hurting person. People in pain and discomfort become like any animal—they need presence and permission to be just as they are. Nothing more.

In my first 10-week group as a "participant" at the cancer center I met Mike, a 23-year-old police officer with stage IV lung cancer. He was a real tough guy, a "man's man." A month before he died, he was bed-ridden, on oxygen, and struggling to breathe.

Seeing someone struggle to breathe is so upsetting. Thirty percent of all the neurons in our bodies are mirror neurons—neurons, that in firing, "mirror" the feelings and behavior of others. It is as though we are experiencing what they are. We can imagine things we've never experienced because we are built to understand other people.

I visited Mike at his home because he could no longer come to us. He wanted to talk about a squirrel that hung out on his window ledge. He started crying and told me how beautiful this creature was, how he'd never cared about squirrels before, but now this one was visiting him every day, and watching it brought him deep joy.

He had accessed a deep love for life itself. He was feeling a kind of rapture that immersed him in gratitude. I was so moved. He was one of the people who ushered me from a life I wanted to get out of into an awareness that life was much more exquisite than I thought it was. A young guy who couldn't breathe could love squirrels! I was starting to realize I'd been missing out on a whole colorful world. I didn't know rapture yet, but I would.

In this 10-week group, we went through the process of imagining the details of our own deaths. Because cancer patients reasonably expend so much energy fearing death, we wanted to give them a chance to rehearse and learn from "the worst" in order to address and release their fears. This way, their energy could be more fully used for healing and living instead. Just as my old therapist Jim had helped me pretend to die when those violent guys in my movie theater dream shot me, the practice of facing dying directly reduced the terror these patients held because they learned they had some choices in how they wanted to die, and they learned through the death rehearsal that dying wasn't actually so unpleasant after all.

In group, following the dying experience, Mike had written that at his actual death, he wanted his brother in bed right next to him and family and friends surrounding him. He didn't want to die alone, but instead he wanted the comfort of lots of people there. Mike's dad and brother didn't know this. His dad wanted to protect Mike from too many visitors, from people seeing him compromised and struggling. He thought of death as a private event. I asked Mike if I could fill them in on his real wishes, and he said Yes.

From that day on, Mike's brother slept in bed with him until Mike died, and Mike's friends could come and go as they pleased. I was told that Mike died in the hospital with all of them there. One of his burly cop friends started crying, and Mike pulled off his oxygen mask to say his last words, *You're ugly,* making all of them laugh and letting them know he was okay. It was Mike's parting gift.

Like Mike, for many cancer patients there comes a time, whether they live or die, when they find the space to respond to cancer rather than primarily reacting to it; when *they* have *it* instead of *it* having *them*. Even though they may still be facing fear and pain and grief, they have stayed open to life itself, and to the difficult path life has given them.

It is this staying open, leaning in, saying Yes to overwhelming difficulty—not necessarily every day, but overall—that creates the most extraordinary transformation. What more can we possibly do in this life?

Life threatening disease forces accelerated growth and change, much of it dreaded and unwelcome at first. For those who can allow transformation to happen, instead of just adaptation, the gifts are precious. For anyone, whether healthy or dying, finding a substantial, consistent, deep Yes to life despite circumstances creates freedom, the kind Viktor found.

Once we find access to loving life and the freedom that comes with it, the natural next thing is to move into responsibility. Freedom without responsibility can be problematic. Being an underachieving teenager drinking whisky instead of going to class is freedom; living on the streets using heroine is freedom; shopping excessively online is freedom—but these acts are devoid of responsibility and sustainable joy.

At the Cancer Center I was learning to care about something beyond my own inner world of suffering. I was discovering that having a sense of responsibility to these cancer patients and their families made me feel better in my life, not worse.

This is what responsibility started to look like for me: once I found compassion and a group of people to be responsible to, I started to really care about my life. I left many of my underachieving ways behind for good. I didn't live on sugar or skip out on work. Instead, I became hungry to learn about the human body, the power of the mind, and what people do in a quest to wake up the human spirit. I read about psychology, philosophy, and spirituality. I studied Joseph Campbell and the "hero's journey." Did I have a hero's journey? Do we all have a hero's journey?

Twenty plus years later, my theoretical orientation is based on looking for sparks of life and meaning in sick and despairing people and building on those. I love helping to identify and highlight what *is* working in a person's life in order to inform and passionately infuse all the places that aren't working.

My superpower is I'm an option-creator. I have a nose for hidden doors that lead to solutions. Give me a bind or a problem, and I'll stay with you there for a while, especially if you've suffered an irretrievable loss. But in the long-term, I don't believe in staying stuck. Being stuck is a self-made, self-perpetuated mindset, and I cannot support that—not in you and not in me.

No matter how insistent my clients can be about a sense of

helplessness or self-righteousness in grievances, I don't believe they ultimately want support for a mindset of despair or "me vs. them." Instead, I believe they are wanting my support to find something true inside of themselves and in the world to be responsible to. In short, they want a life based in meaning.

One client, James, came to me committed to his future suicide. The love of his life had abandoned him, and now he had health complications. Week after week he told me, *There's no point. I just want to die.* Of course we had a suicide contract in place and I fully believed he would honor it (which isn't always the case), so I had some latitude to work with him.

There was nothing reasonable I could say to reach him, so I tossed reason out the window. *Do you see that plant over there?* I asked. *The one on the table?* (That was my first tactic: get him out of his Default Network and into inhabiting his eyes. Remember—it's impossible to be in a story if we are in a Direct Experience.)

Yes, I see it. Nice plant. (He seemed a little annoyed I'd interrupted his misery.)

Before he could get back to discussing his suicide, I said to him, *Well, guess what its name is!*

Still annoyed that I'd stolen the show, he said, *What?*

The plant is named James! Can you believe it? Your name! We have been waiting for you! (Here I'm bringing in magic and love. We needed something beyond the two of us to reach him.)

Guess what James the man did, even though he doesn't believe in magic—he laughed out loud. The suicide trance was broken, for a moment at least. The pattern was briefly disrupted.

Then he went right back to talking about his suicide. *I hate my life; I want to die. Every hour. Every day. I don't know how much longer I'm gonna make it.*

But it was okay because he was still reachable. He was not a lost cause. I just had to continue being strategic and offbeat with him.

A couple of weeks later, on the phone, he asked about James the plant. He had remembered. And I told him a long, true story about how that plant became James—and he laughed out loud some more.

Sometimes he wrote long, middle-of-the-night emails to me about his misery and wishes to be dead. I needed to interrupt this pattern because simply writing the same things over and over wasn't going to help him. I told him he was only allowed to write misery emails to me if he put them in the structure of a sonnet. He laughed at that, too, and he said he would, but he never did.

We went on this way for a long time—three years—before he met a lovely woman and fell madly in love. He texted me after their first date, and I literally did a Snoopy dance! He said, *You were right! I didn't believe you, but you were! I shouldn't have wanted to give up. Thank you for hanging in there with me!* It was my sense of responsibility to him as a suffering person that was the foundation of my commitment to him. Responsibility, I keep learning, is actually an awesome thing!

So there was James, a wealthy and respected man, who could make any choice he wanted. He was an accomplished professional who had published valuable research, and he was admired by many. Still, life hadn't given him what he wanted because one relationship had ended, and he had wanted to use his freedom to turn his back on all of it by choosing death over life.

Do you see how limiting freedom can be when it is not yoked to an equal measure of responsibility? I was struck by the contrast between James's story and my friend Gocho's.

I met Gocho in Addis Ababa. He is a 31-year-old food server at a large hotel who works 48 hours per week and makes $4.24 a day, which comes to $103 per month after taxes. He lives with his brother in a rented 12' x 12' mud house. The toilet and cold-water shower are out back and shared among four families.

I met Gocho on my second trip to Ethiopia and had the privilege of sitting next to him on his very first airplane ride from Addis Ababa to the remote city of Assosa. Like a little kid, he was astonished and joyful at the view above the clouds.

Though Gocho had no medical background, he helped our

American/Ethiopian medical team serve villages in a region that has only one doctor for every one million people. Though life-saving medications cost mere pennies and major surgery costs only $7.00, people there don't have access to the money or transportation to the one small hospital available to them.

Before traveling to Assosa, Gocho believed Addis Ababa was the most poverty-stricken place he could imagine, at least compared to what he had seen on TV. But in Assosa, he was shocked to see even deeper poverty. Many children in this region don't go to school or even have shoes.

Gocho was asked to help treat infected foot wounds. He felt sick to his stomach at the thought and feared he might throw up.

He gathered his courage and practiced the treatment steps on his first patient, an elderly gentleman whose foot was so infected that it was in danger of amputation. *Mix water with hydrogen peroxide in a bucket; place the foot in the bucket and very thoroughly clean the infected wound; dry the foot; put antibacterial ointment on the wound and wrap it carefully; give oral antibiotics.*

This process takes time, and Gocho began asking the man about his life. The man said he lived alone, was lonely, and had no one to care for him. His one son lived hours away in Addis Ababa. He didn't want to leave his land because he feared the government would take it. Gocho listened and gave this man's foot—and his heart—his undivided attention. The man was deeply grateful.

Gocho said his experience with this first patient made him feel blessed and gave him a sense of meaning. He began treating as many wounds as he could. He said, *In wound care, you see exactly what is happening—the infection, the effects of the pain, the response of the people, and then the relief of the people. Being impoverished is difficult enough; being impoverished AND sick is unbearable.*

Becoming responsible to these villagers has changed him. He told me, *Before that, I felt that happiness only came from good things, like TV or entertainment. Since Assosa, I feel so happy. When you do wound care, it is difficult, but you are happy to see their faces after, so happy.*

In the end, Gocho said, *we are human. We help each other and we do the right thing if we can. People don't need to leave their homes and come to Assosa or Ethiopia or Africa; there are families and neighbors back home who also need help.*

Responsibility used to be a bad word to me because it represented a betrayal of my invisible suffering. It was a giving up of my truth. I couldn't move into responsibility before I was ready; I had to connect with and care about something first. Working with cancer patients was that portal for me, and I finally came to understand that responsibility is a precious thing in which being alive and finding meaning intersect.

James and Gocho lived in starkly different emotional worlds. James, in his chronic grief, was out of touch with meaning and trapped in despair; Gocho, poor and overworked, found the joy that meaning affords.

Like Gocho, I had discovered there were people I wanted to serve, and none were more important than my husband and kids. With Claude's help, I realized they were my greatest treasure, and being responsible to them was not a set of shackles, but instead an opportunity with huge payoffs. For too long I had acted as an underachiever with them—drinking too much, traveling too often, and igniting terrible dynamics with Tom.

To my surprise, in facing up to my mistakes and shortcomings, in opening myself to understanding how my mistakes had impacted Tom and our girls, something new was born: a brand new level of commitment to them. In the most unexpected way, bringing a sense of responsibility to my family created a sense of nourishment and joy. Before, I was dominated by avoiding discomfort. As soon as I felt mad or scared, I hopped out of my family, at least in my mind. But with Claude's help in seeing them as my greatest treasure, I began hanging in there to see interactions through even when I was threatened. Responsibility to them became more important than my immediate sense of safety.

Responsibility was the key to my landing in my family for the first time. There were no more exit doors. Responsibility provided grounding and stability. Now Tom, our girls and I could venture into the joy of freedom while at the same time being supported by the nourishing soil of family.

> *Freedom, however, is not the last word. Freedom is only part of the story and half of the truth. Freedom is but the negative aspect of the whole phenomenon whose positive aspect is responsibleness. In fact, freedom is in danger of degenerating into mere arbitrariness unless it is lived in terms of responsibleness.* (Viktor Frankl, *Man's Search for Meaning*, p. 132)

To Viktor, responsibility was such an important partner to freedom that he wanted to build a Statue of Responsibility on the West Coast to partner with the Statue of Liberty on the East Coast.

Questions for Reflection:

1. Which responsibilities in your life infringe upon your freedom? Which responsibilities support your freedom?
2. It's easy to associate freedom with joy. To what degree are you able to connect responsibility with joy?
3. Describe a time when freedom did not accompany responsibility in your life and you suffered for it?
4. Describe a time when you were immersed in responsibility and felt deep freedom and joy at the same time?

Actions to Immediately Increase Your Life Force:

1. Identify a responsibility that is meaningful to you (such as raising your kids or working on a project or serving a community). In this moment, feel your sense of responsibility

on one hand and the freedom associated with your role on the other hand; enjoy the interplay of the two.

2. Think of a responsibility that burdens you. Actively look for a way either to free yourself from the burden (like quitting something you don't really want to do) or a meaningful outcome if you stay committed to the burdensome responsibility. In other words, find a way to add freedom either by stopping or by expanding your view of the outcome.

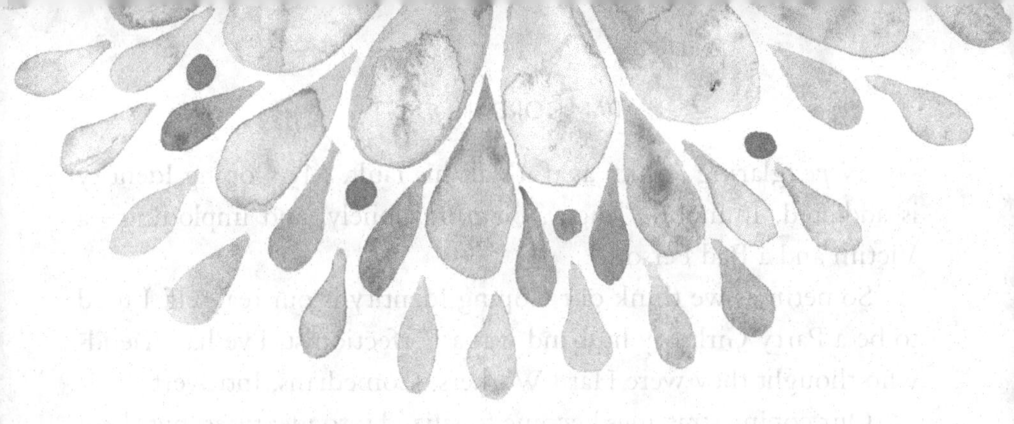

Chapter 8

FUTURE SELF WISDOM (VS. UNCONSCIOUS HABITS)

We all have a Coping Identity and an Essence Identity.

Our Coping Identity comes from our Default Network and reacts in a patterned way. When stressed or freaked out, it eats certain foods, breathes and tenses up in habitual ways, and says special repetitive phrases. It has a narrow focus on a tiny, upsetting aspect of life. It's trapped in a small world.

My mom ate Saltines with butter and paced around the kitchen muttering, *Oh, I'm so stupid—I hate myself!* Maybe she'd forgotten an appointment or dropped a dish. A little mistake ruined her sense of herself. That was her Coping Identity—a stupid screwup.

When I'm in my Coping Identity, I make a cup of coffee and sit down on the couch to play *Bubble Cloud* or *2048* on my phone. I can stay there for hours with my shoulders tense and my face furled. My Coping Identity becomes only interested in mastering new levels of my game and getting high scores. I'm sucked in and while I play, my mind ruminates on "All the Terrible Things" that are going to ruin my life.

Two to three hours later, if Tom asks me *What's up?* I might say, *Things are all messed up.* He'll ask, *Do you want to talk about it?* I'll say, *Nope,* glaring at him as if it's all his fault. My Coping Identity is addicted, immobile, angry, blaming, lonely, and imploding—a Victim and a Bad Person.

Sometimes we think our Coping Identity is our real self. I used to be a Party Girl. My husband was a Perfectionist. I've had friends who thought they were Hard Workers, Comedians, Introverts.

Our coping strategies become fossilized into identities, but these identities reduce us into far less than we really are.

Your Essence Identity, by contrast, is the expansive, loving you that is open to many possibilities. The walls between yourself and the larger world crumble. You naturally belong; you breathe easily; you're engaged in the moment at hand. You notice the beautiful sunset and forget for a moment that you're separate from it (perhaps you aren't, but that's another discussion!). You smile at your child for being so cute, and you lose any sense of separateness as you beam. When we're in our Essence Identity, we merge in a beautiful way with life in front of us.

If coping knows only *Me, Me, Me*, then essence knows *We.*

A quick way to get in touch with your Essence Identity is to ask yourself, *At what times in my life did I feel most alive? When have I experienced Heaven on Earth?* Answers will bubble up, and you'll remember occasions when you had access to expansion.

I led some one-day Meaning Workshops because I wanted to share with the community what I was discovering about meaning and expansiveness.

Rose attended. A popular swim school owner, she told the group she had a broken heart. As she described it, her fingers touched the skin around her heart, and her face looked grieved, despairing. John, the love of her life, had suffered a debilitating brain injury in a terrible cycling accident six months earlier. He couldn't walk without assistance, used a feeding tube for meals, and required a caregiver 24/7 for basic functioning.

I asked Rose, *Can you share a memory of when life felt particularly meaningful?* She thought for a minute, smiled, and told the group what happened on their recent five-year wedding anniversary. Rose dug her wedding dress out of the closet, put it on, fixed her makeup and hair, and even fastened the veil. When she walked into the bedroom and surprised John, his face lit up. Then he had his caregiver find his tux, dress him in it, shave, and fix his hair. Using a walker, John joined Rose in the hallway, where they had a photo shoot—including pretending to drink champagne.

Rose began laughing and beaming as she shared this story.

Where do you feel this meaningful memory in your body? I asked. *I feel warm in my heart, and it's spreading out,* she said using her hands to show us. Meaning is often a full-bodied experience.

Next, I asked the key question, which is a trick because it bypasses the Default Network: *Is there a message from the warmth and expansion in your heart to your broken heart?*

For a moment she looked confused, and then her eyes widened in surprise. *Yes. It says to my heart, "You're not broken."* We all laughed and cried because we all knew it was true. She had gone from coping to essence in five minutes.

In that workshop, Rose lit up all six areas of meaning with her story. After she initiated a celebration with John (creativity) and they saw each other in their wedding outfits (experiences), Rose created a memory that would touch their lives, and all our lives as well (history). Being playful and generous (attitude), she taught us how we might approach hard times (legacy). And, of course, she showed John that she loved him (love!). This is an essence story.

Just as moment by moment we choose miracle or grievance, moment by moment we choose essence or coping. It's the same thing. This can serve as your compass.

A teacher once told me, *Coping Identities have crises; Essence Identities do not.* I searched for scenarios to question this assertion. *What if someone rejects me? What if my daughters are treated badly or get injured? What if . . .* But my body took a breath, one of those deep ones, and it recognized the sound of truth. Coping Identities have crises and Essence Identities do not. I ultimately have a choice between them, and so do you—always.

Viktor knew this when he said, *Every human being has the freedom to change at any instant.* (*Man's Search for Meaning,* p. 131)

What do Coping and Essence Identities have to do with the future? Everything. If we don't know better, we roam through life in our Default Networks, and over time our Coping Identities solidify. We may passively hope for life to get better without knowing that we are the ones who must create better. In doing so, the future is our friend.

At this very moment, we all have a Future Self who knows much more than we do about the most meaningful direction we can take in any area of our life. Our Future Self is connected to our essence even as our current self struggles with coping. We need to talk to this wise Future Self to find a better way.

Let's start small. It's late at night, you're bummed, and you're considering having a strong drink or calling your ex or wolfing down another bag of chips. Ask yourself, *How do I want to feel when I wake up in the morning?* Your Future Self will tell you the truth. My Future Self always wants me to wake up with energy for the day ahead; she never wants me groggy or embarrassed or compromised.

On the Friday nights before I headed to Orinda to train on my bike for the AIDS Ride, I lived like a saint. I ate a big, healthy dinner, avoided dessert and alcohol, hydrated, and got plenty of sleep. I wanted to be at my best because the next day mattered so much to me.

If you have a big event coming—a presentation or a sports event or a trip—ask your Future Self how you want to feel at that event.

Physically strong? Prepared? Clearheaded? Your Future Self will know—and it may even share additional information with you!

But every day matters, so we can ask our future selves for help on normal days, too.

The first year I volunteered with UC Davis Camp Kesem, I just knew I would fall in love with the 100 college kids who generously volunteered as camp counselors. I didn't even know them yet, but I chose one of my favorite poems—*The Invitation* by Oriah Mountain Dreamer—and made copies on pretty paper for all of them. I read it out loud at the end-of-camp party.

I want to know
if you can live with failure
yours and mine
and still stand on the edge of the lake
and shout to the silver of the full moon,
"Yes!"

Sharing this poem was a gift from my essence to theirs, a wish for their lives to be expansive and based in love, not fear.

My Future Self told me to do that.

You can ask your Future Self open-ended questions. Go to a quiet place and ask good quality questions. *What do I really want? Am I headed in the right direction? What do I need to let go of?*

You can make your Future Self as old as you want to: a year older, 10 years older, even 50!

My 75-year-old Future Self is super smart; she's got her priorities dialed in. If it weren't for her, I wouldn't even be writing this book! Talking with her is like talking with God—I can ask her anything!

Future Self, should I exercise today?

Oh yes. Exercise is invigorating! Get outside and enjoy the fresh air! She has no hesitation.

Future Self, my friend's husband died. What should I do?

Just be there; the best you can do is be there. You'll lose important things someday, and what will matter most is people being there. Being there is always the thing to do.

But I haven't seen her in years. What if she's mad at me?

No matter, just go to her; she needs people to be there to remind her this world is still a place to which she belongs.

Future Self, I didn't like how that meeting went. Should I bring it up, perhaps write an email about it?

No, don't waste your energy. Instead do something you enjoy. When you're my age, that meeting won't matter at all—you won't even remember it—but doing things you enjoy always matters!

My Future Self is also good for avoiding possible mistakes. At a fork in the road, she knows what to do and why. Viktor had some insight into this:

> *Live as if you were living already for the second time and as if you had acted the first time as wrongly as you are about to act now! It seems to me that there is nothing which would stimulate a man's sense of responsibleness more than this maxim, which invites him to imagine first that the present is past and, second, that the past may yet be changed and amended.* (*Man's Search for Meaning,* p. 109)

One time, when Viktor was getting beaten up by SS guards, he imagined himself in the future, lecturing on the psychology of a concentration camp. This gave him a reason to endure and learn from the moment at hand—and from all such moments—for the purpose of creating a meaningful future.

As Nietzsche said, *If we know our why, we can manage any how.*

When my friend Cynthia was 46, she was diagnosed with an aggressive form of leukemia, and she didn't see how she could survive. She decided to undergo four consecutive, potentially dangerous clinical trials for her cancer. She wanted to help science help her daughters if they were to develop this cancer, too.

Even when she had an anaphylactic allergic reaction to one of the drugs in the first trial and could have died, Cynthia continued because she had a reason to go forward; she had a *why.* Her *why* brought her through experiences of nausea, vomiting, bone pain, fatigue from the treatments, and many trips to the ER. She also told me later that because many people—including her dear sister-in-law, who died of pancreatic cancer at the age of 47—never have a shot at a cure, Cynthia felt it would be immoral not to participate in a clinical trial when so many others don't get a chance. Another *why.*

Miraculously, these trials ended up saving her life, and her Future Self led the way.

Bingo, a Camp Kesem counselor, studied for the MCATs 14 hours every day last summer. I was in awe of his tenacity and dedication, and a little jealous. Why didn't I have that power of focus? Why did he? I asked him about it, and he said, *When I get tired of studying, I think of my future patients and do it for them.* Whoa. He's only 22 and already tapping into the power of his Future Self, riding on the love and generosity of his essence. I was excited to write a letter of recommendation to medical schools for him, and I included this amazing story. Who wouldn't want this guy in their program? I'm so happy for his future patients.

I have a coach who tells me all challenges are actually "worthy opponents" that carry hidden opportunities, and that we reap their gifts in the future. We can even intentionally create worthy opponents for our future selves.

Cynthia and I learned about an exciting trend called Transformational Travel, which are vacations designed for growth and discovery. These journeys push us out of our comfort zones and return us home feeling healthier, more present, and more inspired—not depleted, not hungover, and not more overweight.

We have begun leading groups to Spain and Japan to walk on an ancient pilgrimage route to experience a transformational journey among a growth-minded group of new friends. The Camino de Santiago in northern Spain and the Kumano Kodo in southern Japan provide settings for back-to-back days of walking while unwinding, opening, and hearing the deeper inner voice that gets buried in our habits and busyness.

Like a prayer for the future, a modern pilgrimage is an act of faith that if a person lets go of the world they know for a time and walks in a new place, both alone and in the company of people from all over the world, by the end of the journey they will become more aligned with their authentic, vital selves. They will recognize the voice and wisdom of their Future Self more quickly than they could at home.

I've started inviting people in a transition who call me for therapy sessions to join us on a pilgrimage instead.

I'm stuck. I'm grieving and need a way to honor my experience. I'm an empty nester and don't even know who I am without my kids. I'm going through a messy divorce. Everyone thinks I'm fine now that my cancer is gone, but I don't feel fine. I don't hear pathology and diagnoses in these stories, but I hear a need for connection to meaning in the midst of a transition. I hear a vital identity challenge: *Who am I now that . . .*

A walk in an unfamiliar place puts people in touch with Direct Experience, the healthy network in our brains that is open to growth rather than hunkered down in survival mode. New neural pathways are built, while a safe community of people provides emotional scaffolding.

Because we only grow outside of our comfort zones, we must find the courage to try unfamiliar experiences in order to awaken new possibilities in our lives.

It was in preparing for the AIDS Ride that I realized, to my surprise, that I actually am an athlete. Before that event, I'd only admired athletes from the sidelines.

Here is more good news about your Future Self: the people you admire right now embody qualities that you already have inside you. These qualities may seem foreign to you now, but they are in there, and they are clues to your essence. They are waiting to be identified and developed.

If you admire athletes like I did, guess what: you are an athlete in disguise (disguised by the trappings of your Coping Identity!). If you admire good parents, you have the makings of a good mother or father in you. If you admire perseverance, you have truckloads of it right inside you. Why would we be attracted to something that we don't already have inside of us? We may not be living it yet, but it's in there! Visualize who you would be with the qualities you admire. What dreams are you avoiding that could become realities if you only watered some seeds that are already inside of you?

Recently, I was in Cambodia on an adventurous tour. I woke up early one morning to see two men from my group doing lunges along the edge of the pool. *What the hell?! Weren't they getting enough exercise all day long with the rest of us?* Watching their drive and dedication, I immediately felt bad about myself: *Why don't I have drive like that? What do they understand that I don't?!*

Aside from the AIDS ride, it was my pattern to conserve my energy as much as possible. I wanted to accomplish more in my life, to support dreams of writing, connecting, and creating, but I didn't have habits in place to work harder. Instead, I rested as much as I could between clients and tasks. This isn't so unusual—some rest is important—but since there was a gap between how I was living and my dreams, I needed something to change. Gaps between our coping patterns and our essence are painful! But I dreaded the thought of using more energy in my life—where would I find it?

The guys doing lunges had found extra energy—I could tell. They had the determination and grit I admired. I was about to learn that conserving energy doesn't make energy. Spending energy makes energy.

I approached them and asked what they were doing. They were very excited about Andy Frisella's *MFCEO Project* Podcast and a challenge called *75HARD*. The purpose is to increase mental toughness by doing five things each day for 75 consecutive days without one cheat or error, and if you mess up you must start all over again.

The point is not to change your body, though that will happen. The point is to cultivate mental strength. Succeeding in this challenge doesn't depend on physical ability; it's about the power of the mind. Doing these five things, especially on the hardest days, is what skyrockets your capacity to build your dreams.

I was ready to awaken mental toughness in me. I wanted to enter my future as someone more capable than I thought I was. I needed to know, finally, that I could do anything I committed to.

I started the five things on May 13, 2019 and finished on July 27. I did it. Now, a month later, I'm finishing this book. These two events are entirely connected. By committing to a practice of discipline for 75 days in a row, I learned to say Yes to actions even when my Coping Identity tried to pull me to the couch. Day after day I won the battle between the Yes of my essence and the No of my fear. The strength in listening to the "right inner voice," the one who cares about my best life, translated to writing this book and to other meaningful activities, like going the extra mile at work or with my family, even when I was tired.

My Future Self knew I had mental strength. We all do in our essence. But I didn't know it as clearly as I do now, after having stuck with the strict program for 75 days straight.

If you want to try this challenge, here's what you do:

1. Pick and stick to a diet of your choice; no cheating and no alcohol. I went off sugar, gluten, and corn—that meant I could still eat french fries!
2. Complete two 45-minute workouts every day, and at least one of them has to be outside regardless of the weather.

3. Drink one gallon of water each day (based on my body weight and some blood work partway through, I found I needed a little less).
4. Read 10 pages of self-improvement non-fiction each day; read actively (underline important passages). Read a book—listening to Audible doesn't count.
5. Take a selfie each day to document your progress.

This challenge restores trust in yourself. When trust breaks down, we get mentally weak. When we say we are changing our habits and we don't, we betray ourselves and the mountain ahead of us grows larger. When we follow through with integrity, we get stronger. *75HARD* is about giving birth to the future you. It's about awakening your potential.

Be careful, though. If you tap into the wisdom of your Future Self and take on a challenge such as walking the Camino de Santiago or doing *75HARD*, you might begin to feel more joy than you're used to, and sustained joy can be scary. Our survival brains aren't built for letting our guards down in this way!

In *The Big Leap,* Gay Hendricks taught about something he calls the *Upper Limit Problem.* We humans are so wired for danger that when we start to feel sustained joy—when we approach our upper limit of joy—it's easy for us to sabotage ourselves because the survival brain can't risk exposing us to danger by going off-duty for long. To thwart feeling good we might break a toe or wreck our car or eat 20 cookies or start a fight with our beloved—anything to restore the brain to its quest for safety in a harsh world.

Hendricks says we must train ourselves to sustain our joy for longer and longer amounts of time (that is, increase our upper limit) because sustained joy is so unnatural to us on a biological and evolutionary level.

"Upper Limit Problem" became my phrase of choice when I

learned about it, and my husband and daughters began to echo it back to me, which I appreciated.

I'd be feeling good, and without realizing it, I'd try to ruin it by starting an argument. I might say, *Tom, why do you never bring me flowers anymore? I've told you a million times I love flowers and you never give me any. It's not that hard.*

Hon, he'd say, *are you having an upper limit problem?*

Ha ha ha. Yes, in fact, I am. Thank you.

Or I might say, *Lauren, can you please not put your wet towel on the carpet? It's gross. Mildew will grow and the whole house will smell like mildew and we'll all get sick.*

Upper limit problem, Mom!!

Okay, fine. You're probably right.

Miracle or Grievance? Essence Identity or Coping Identity? Sustained Joy or Upper Limit Problem? Your Future Self is waiting to help.

Questions for Reflection:

1. How would you describe your Coping Identity? What patterns of coping with stress does it use?
2. When is a time you connected with your Essence Identity? Remember everything you saw, heard, felt, and believed. What would your life be like if you could access that mindset whenever you wanted?
3. Think of a memory when life felt particularly meaningful. What sensations do you feel in your body as you remember? What is the strongest sensation? What message might this strongest sensation have for a current challenge in your life?
4. What would your 90-year-old self say about your current life? Listen without defensiveness. Ask this Future Self, "What else?"

Actions to Immediately Increase Your Life Force:

1. Take your Future Self out to coffee and interview them. Add 20 or more years to their life and see if your older Future Self is even smarter! Share three current challenges and ask your older Future Self for advice. Take notes on their answers. Stay curious.
2. Begin the mental toughness challenge, *75HARD*, using the original program or one that works for you. Tell trusted friends you're doing it and ask them to join you or cheer you on.

Chapter 9

UNCONDITIONAL LOVE (VS. AGAINST-NESS)

When Viktor got out of the camps, he returned to his home, Vienna, where he lived among Jews and families of SS guards. Some people saw him as a sellout for being willing to live among Nazis. They believed his association with them was the same as condoning them. He told a story of one woman who had criticized him for speaking German, the language of Hitler. Viktor asked her, *Do you use kitchen knives? Yes, of course,* she said. *Well, how could you,* he asked, *when so many have been murdered with knives?* (Viktor Frankl, *Man's Search for Meaning,* p. 150)

Even after all he lost and suffered, and perhaps because of all he lost and suffered, he refused to be against any group of people. He said that there are two kinds of people in the world: decent and indecent.

> *Both are found everywhere; they penetrate into all groups of society. No group consists entirely of decent or indecent people—and therefore one occasionally found a decent fellow among the camp guards.* (*Man's Search for Meaning,* p. 86)

After the war, Viktor believed that if he could relate to the guards and help them open to their humanity, then the world would be better a better place. Being for every person is what dignity does. Viktor didn't forget or minimize the wrongs done to him, but he believed in a person's ability to make productive choices and take responsibility for them.

I admire people who fight for the betterment of *all* people, not just some. It's an important distinction that being for all people does not mean being for all situations. I wanted to learn how to not be against others, too. I admired Viktor's position in theory, but I only felt open to everyone on days when the sun was shining and people were kind to me.

With the turn of a mood, I could catapult into all kinds of "against-ness": against my parents, against my biological family, against various people I'd had conflicts with, against the lady with the angry face at the grocery store who was clearly against me—or at least not *for* me.

I had an extra bad beginning in my life, and a very lonely middle. How much could one person actually change in a lifetime, and what would it take? As Jim had said, I had an abandonment and betrayal story. I didn't want to have that story; it was just there, like a cement block that wouldn't budge. I had thoughts such as, *Maybe this just isn't my lifetime to figure out how to be for all people.* My life had too much pain arising from the outside and not enough capacity for coping on the inside.

In the oldest, wisest part of me knew the truth; I couldn't actually find a single person on this planet whom I could justify being against. I also knew that as soon as I started being against anyone, I was lost. But my nervous system and the patterns of my survival brain were so entrenched that when under "threat," I put up my shield and fired shots, at least in my mind.

I began to seriously study how to stop being against anyone. I turned my refrigerator into a collage of forgiveness quotes:

A magnet read, *I forgive your confusion.* I think the Buddha said that.

A paragraph by the Dalai Lama about being against what the Chinese *did*, but not against the Chinese *themselves,* was taped above it.

Taped to the right was the following story:

> *An old Cherokee grandfather is telling his grandson a story. "A fight is going on inside me," he said." It is a terrible fight between two wolves. One is evil — he is anger, envy, greed, arrogance, resentment, lies, and ego. The other is good — he is joy, peace, love, hope, serenity, humility, kindness, empathy, generosity, truth, compassion, and faith. The wolves are fighting to the death." Wide-eyed, the boy asks his grandfather which wolf will win. The grandfather simply replied, "The one I feed."*

Below that a large magnet simply read, *Breathe.*

I studied forgiveness to learn how to stop having grievances. Especially helpful was *Forgive For Good* by Fred Luskin, director of the Stanford University Forgiveness Projects. "Against" was killing me—I lived with a feeling of twisting tension in my chest night and day, so I read his book like my life depended on it. I learned that to form a grievance we have to do specific things: we take a normal life event and make it *very personal* (rather than seeing it as something that just happened), and then we exaggerate how important it is. Next, we ruminate about it and stop looking at it from new perspectives. As a result, we get stuck, and our perspective becomes fossilized as "The Truth."

This recipe for a grievance called me out in a way that made me laugh out loud when I read it. I laughed first because the thought of me exaggerating the centrality of my role in a grievance was embarrassing. And second, I laughed out of pure relief that if my grievance wasn't, in fact, so personal, that meant I wasn't so bad.

All this research was my attempt to stop suffocating from a lifetime of against-ness in me. From the time I can remember, that cannon had swung both ways: the world was against me, and as soon as something went wrong, I was against the world.

Two years ago, my friend Cynthia and I went on our first weeklong silent meditation retreat. I was tired of listening to kids and clients; too many words were relentlessly bombarding my poor ears. I needed some quiet and rest. I needed to be off duty.

All talking and eye contact stopped after dinner on the first night. It was only then that I learned this was a "metta retreat." Metta is the Pali word for friendship and lovingkindness, and it's a very *active* form of mediation practice. I realized I'd have to work the whole time during this retreat after all, and I was pissed.

Aside from some walking meditation, chores, qigong, and sleeping, all we did for seven straight days from 6 a.m. to 9 p.m. was metta meditation.

A silent prayer, metta goes something like this:

> *May you be happy.*
> *May you be healthy and strong in your body.*
> *May you be safe and protected from danger.*
> *May you have ease.*

The first day we started by focusing on a person we could offer these words to without reservation. I chose Joey, my daughter's Italian Greyhound; he was the only "person" I could think of for whom my heart felt completely pure.

As I sat on a cushion in a large meditation hall with a hundred other silent people, I imagined little Joey and repeated the mantra over and over, trying to feel it.

Joey, may you be happy. . . . Yep, I meant this.

Joey, may you be healthy and strong in your body. . . . God, yes. I never want Joey to suffer!

Joey, may you be safe and protected from danger. . . . Yes, for sure. Oh, I couldn't bear to lose Joey.

Joey, may you have ease. . . . Yes, I want ease for Joey. Always.

My heart was fully aligned with this metta practice. Not a bone in my body was in any way against Joey.

After I'd spent about six hours with Joey, we had to shift our focus to another person. Oh, God, here we go. Next up was Tom, my dear husband. But you know how hard marriage is, right? He's screwed me over a zillion times, and I've done the same to him. I could feel conditions arising within me: what if I became less against him than he was against me? Wouldn't I be in danger? Wouldn't I be a fool?

Tom, may you be happy. . . . Well, if you love me enough and you're not being a jerk to me, happy is fine. I don't want to wish you well if you're not going to wish me the same. May you be happy IF . . .

Tom, may you be healthy and strong, and safe and protected. . . . Yes. I'm not a total bitch.

Tom, may you have ease. . . . Well yeah, if it makes you a better husband. Ease IF . . .

After hours and hours of focusing on Tom, it got easier. My heart softened around the edges of IF until there was just a mist of an IF, and then it blew away. I was fully on board with these four wishes for Tom, no matter what he did or didn't do for me. My mental battle had left the building, and briefly only my heart remained on the meditation cushion, with no conditions.

Next we focused on someone we have mixed feelings toward. Not an enemy, just a mixed bag. I picked a couple of hard clients. My mental struggle was back with me on the cushion, wagging its finger, holding its ground.

May you be happy. . . . Yeah, then you'll leave therapy!

May you be healthy, strong, safe, and protected. . . . Yes, of course.

May you have ease. . . . Okay, fine, we all deserve ease. Couldn't you just make my life easier?

Over and over I rehearsed the prayer, until the conditions left, and I began to feel pure compassion for these people. Memories flooded in of funny moments we'd shared, triumphs they'd celebrated. My heart opened to compassion for how they were trying their best. *Whoa! This stuff works!* I thought.

On day four, we were to focus on an enemy. It could be a political figure, an ex. I chose my birth family, the whole lot of them.

May you be happy. . . . I straight up disassociated.

May you be healthy and strong. . . . Maybe.

May you be safe. . . . Probably.

May you have ease. . . . Nope, too unfair.

My birth family was my biggest, oldest, deepest challenge. Not *them* really, but the ways they made me feel. Or the way life made me feel. Or just the way I felt. Or...

I practiced again and again:

May you be happy.

May you be healthy and strong in your body.

May you be safe and protected from danger.

May you have ease.

After some time, the tension left me, and I didn't die from letting it go. There was scaffolding in me! All the work I'd done provided me with stability as I slew that gigantic dragon of against-ness inside me. We could inhabit this earth together, my birth family and I. Oh, the relief!

But I had more work to do.

Instead of doing a 30-minute walking meditation where you very slowly and mindfully step back and forth along a 10-foot-long line, I walked a quarter mile to the edge of the property to visit a horse eating hay in the middle of his pen. I'd been off sugar and working hard in silence for four days now, and everything in me felt clearer and purer, like I was hearing a single flute playing a melody instead of five radio stations all blaring at once.

I stood by the fence and willed the horse to come over to me. His big brown eyes blinked just a foot from mine, and I was astonished at the beauty of his large pupils and lashes. At age 52, I was truly *seeing* a horse for the very first time. Surely we had a spiritual bond, and, as in equine therapy, he was mirroring my inner peacefulness, right?

After dinner, I walked back out to see the horse. I was certain he'd remember me and come right over. But he didn't. He just stayed in the middle of the pen, ignoring my click click clicks and kiss kiss kisses. *Fuck you,* I thought. *Here I am, lonely and having sugar withdrawal, and you're the only one I can look at directly, and you'd rather stand alone in the middle of your pen than hang out by the fence with me! Harrumph. I don't even know if I'm going to come see you again tomorrow!* I turned away from the horse while I rolled my eyes at my ridiculous self and walked back, hating everything again.

That night I did my metta practice with the horse.

May you be happy. . . . Yeah, okay.

May you be healthy and strong. . . .Yeah, fine.

May you have ease. . . .Yes.

As I stayed with my metta prayer for the horse, my heart opened, and I thought about how I could love the horse without any expectations, without any conditions. I could visit him tomorrow and practice loving him just as he is, no matter what he wants to do. I could practice feeling the honor of just being in his company, just being near his beauty. That's what I did the rest of the week. The horse became my teacher. He walked over to me sometimes, but that didn't matter anymore.

As I continued to practice unconditional love, I wondered how far I could take it.

Could I not be against spiders? Mold? What about rape and murder? Well, those are actions, not beings. Rapists? Murderers? Maybe, perhaps if I understood how they got that way. White supremacists? School shooters? I began working on these.

The point isn't to neutralize or condone anyone or anything that harms. The point is to understand what being against other people does to us! Against-ness breeds more against-ness, both inside of us and around us.

Most of us have plenty of "reason" to be against many people—real people in our lives, people in the political sphere, and cultural symbols of evil like Nurse Ratchet and Freddy Krueger. Our survival brains are in us, 24/7, ready to turn against a threat, so the easiest thing to do with evil and harm is to turn against the people who cause them.

Rapists separate us from safety. Murderers separate us from life. Liars separate us from truth. Racists separate us from dignity. We easily turn against people who are *against.*

But this act of turning against costs us dearly and taxes all the major systems of our bodies. Being against rings an alarm bell of crisis, emergency, even fear for our very survival. It's a taxing, full-bodied experience.

Remember how my dad shunned me? I spent hours and precious health on him. I remember for years as a child trying to sleep but having a rapid pulse, shallow breathing, tense muscles, and chronic revenge fantasies. The hate within me afflicted my young body. Hate is a full-time job, and with my hate in charge, I unintentionally compromised my power to do anything constructive or satisfying in the world. Punishing him punished me.

At Esalen, I watched Bob Thurman, a Buddhist, talk about sin. I've never been interested in sin; my adoptive parents were atheists, so we didn't even believe in sin. Why was everyone so riled up about the Ten Commandments? I couldn't name them if I tried, although I'm sure I've broken most of them.

Bob Thurman told us that the basis of all sin is separation, that sin separates us from each other. If you tell someone a lie, you are giving them a false picture of reality, and that separates them from you. Separation . . . Sin. When I heard this, I suddenly felt more respect for the Bible. Maybe the ancients understood far more than I was just beginning to understand.

My life started in separation—from my mother, father, original name, lineage, relatives, siblings, history, traditions, culture, and heroic ancestors. My search for non-separation, for unconditional love and belonging, has been like a 40-year crawl through desert sands. Searching for non-separation, for unconditional love, has become my greatest quest.

I want my heart to feel so full of love that when I have a problem, rather than turning against, my first questions are, *How do I add more love to this situation?* and *What would love do?* I really want this.

My friend from Ethiopia told me a common proverb in his country: *To forgive is to set a prisoner free and realize that prisoner was you.*

Maybe you have an active survival brain like I do, one that continuously scours the environment for enemies, hatred, and threats to your survival. I went to Tony Robbins' Date with Destiny last year and learned that my primary question in life—the biggest question under all other questions for all of my life—has been, *How do I protect myself?* Realizing that was both a shocker and also the most normal thing in the world. When I look at every single one of my failures—failure to keep a relationship, failure to be kind, failure to achieve, failure to do the right thing—they are all grounded in this fundamental question: *How do I protect myself?* Ninety-nine percent of the time it's not a good question.

The opposite orientation, the orientation based in Unconditional Love, says, *Shut up, survival brain. You can't always protect yourself. Sometimes you're gonna get hurt and you can handle getting hurt. It'll be worth it. We have bigger fish to fry in this life.*

Banishing against-ness does not weaken our causes, but rather strengthens our ability to support our causes! When we are caught in the traps of resentment and hatred, we are much less capable of effectively addressing real problems in the world. Our survival brains are not creative creatures. They unwittingly pour gasoline instead of water on fires. They waste energy and detract from real change.

Anger is powerful fuel for change, but anger is not the same as resentment or hate. Anger simply means, *I don't like this.* A mama grizzly bear "doesn't like it" when someone goes near her cubs. Anger can be directed intelligently. Many of the world's most effective agents of change worked within the system to change it. They became part of something they didn't agree with, and they worked their asses off to make institutions more equitable and fair.

Ruth Bader Ginsberg is a hero because she worked her entire career to eliminate gender inequality in legislation and regulations. To do that, she had to go to law school as virtually the only woman in her class. She had to rise to the top of her class while raising a baby and taking care of her sick husband. There is no doubt that she experienced sexism at Harvard, but she kept her sight on the larger goal. She suffered and endured with a sense of meaning.

Not all of us can go to Harvard Law School, but we can learn from RBG's attitude, and the attitude of others like her, to effect change in our own lives and communities. To most effectively do this, we cannot reject the people who make us angry and who act unfairly. We have to get smarter than the alarms of our two-million-year-old brains.

I don't think about my adoptive parents or my biological families much anymore. When I do, tension and heat don't accompany the thoughts. I don't need my past to be different. I don't need my family members to be different. What's happened is I've become far more interested in something else: How I can serve the most people in my life now that I'm finally invested in being here? This is my new primary question.

I've been realizing, sometimes with astonishment, that it does feel better to love. I have less addiction, less stress, and less brain fog when I love. I have more energy, an easier smile, and more frequent synchronicities when I love. I'm talking about love without reservation, wholehearted love, unconditional love. Not loving every action, but loving every being.

> *Love is the only way to grasp another human being in the innermost core of his personality. No one can become fully aware of the very essence of another human being unless he loves him.* (Viktor Frankl, *Man's Search for Meaning*, p. 111)

For you:

> *May you be happy.*
> *May you be healthy and strong in your body.*
> *May you be safe and protected from danger.*
> *May you have ease.*

Questions for Reflection:

1. What grievances do you live with? What do they cost you in terms of peace, health, self-esteem, and joy?
2. What would your life feel like without any grievances at all? What would you do with all the energy that would return to you?
3. Who are the hardest groups of people to not be against? What do you fear you would lose if you were not against them?
4. How could you address justice and maintain high standards for behavior while at the same time not turning against others? Is it possible?

Actions to Immediately Increase Your Life Force:

1. Choose a person you have a grievance against and practice metta meditation with them in mind. Practice it with yourself in mind, too. Don't worry if you don't feel a benefit right away. Just keep doing it.
2. Decide what you would like your new primary question in life to be, and write it someplace where you will see it often—in your day-planner, on a sticky note on your mirror or dashboard, on your screensaver. Feel the pleasant alignment with your essence in exploring your new primary question.

Chapter 10

"SPECTACULAR" COMMUNITY (VS. ISOLATION)

When I was seven, I built an elevator to the stars in my parents' coat closet. Once I entered, I stood in front of the coats with my nose nearly touching the door. To my right, I had taped a crayon-colored control panel with buttons to take me up, up, up and out of there, flying toward my real home.

I spent a lot of time in that elevator, trying to reach the people I belonged to on my home planet. I'd hear my mom walking past the closet, calling, *Pamela, where are you?* When I was sure she had passed me, I'd slip out and deal with whatever she needed and then slip right back inside, returning to my most important mission: finding my people.

When I was a young adult, I thought finding my biological family was the key to making me whole. In my fantasy, our severed relationship had been a terrible mistake, and there was a very good explanation for it all: I'd been stolen or switched at the hospital. I fantasized that my biological family had gathered an army of volunteers, detectives, and scent hounds at a community center. They'd hung posters and offered rewards to anyone who could help them heal the hole in their hearts by recovering me. But in reality I was the only one searching.

I eventually met most of my biological family, and some meetings were okay, but I didn't feel whole from knowing them. Instead, I felt the ongoing shocks of how much I didn't truly belong to them and never had.

A community is a group of people who feel they belong to each other. Who did I belong to? And who belonged to me? I've been working on these questions for decades, and my recent visit to Cambodia offered me some clarity.

During the Cambodian genocide, the Khmer Rouge killed nearly two million people, almost a quarter of the country. When their rule ended, still more people died from diseases, landmines, and starvation. A more accurate number for the death toll may be three million, an entire generation. The impact continues to affect everyone there today.

In the spring of 2019, I traveled to Cambodia with a group and a spiritual teacher, Panache Desai. We visited S-21, which is now the Tuol Sleng Genocide Museum. It had once been a school, but when the war started, it was turned into a prison and a place of torture. As many as 17,000 men, women, and children were detained and killed there. Panache counseled us to stay open to the emotions we felt, to let them flow through us. Even though it's still hard for me to cry, I was ready to try my best to remain open.

We met Chum Mey, an 89-year-old man and one of only two remaining survivors of the prison. As a young man he had watched his wife and baby son be shot and killed. He still has nightmares, but he returns to S-21 every day to tell the world what happened there.

He showed us scars on his body, and he told us stories of being electroshocked and having his toenails ripped out. His purpose in life is to share these stories to honor the dead and to help all of us understand, with the hope that these atrocities will never happen again. This is what gets him up in the morning; this is his gift to the world.

I felt a nearly unbearable heaviness at that prison. Barbed wire surrounded us, and inside the buildings were hundreds of photos showing terrified and despairing faces. I followed Panache's directive to stay open, and I felt heartbroken. I felt as though I was wearing one of those heavy lead aprons used during dental x-rays. *Relax your body,* I told myself. *Let yourself cry; crying is honest.*

Next we went to the Killing Fields where we saw mass graves and a giant tree where children had been tortured. We saw a temple of human skulls, meant to show the world the brutality of what had occurred there. *Relax,* I told myself. *Don't trap the pain inside; let it come up. Nothing bad will happen if you cry in front of people. No one will hurt you.*

With shock and the heaviness of grief, we left the sites. At lunch, we met Scott Neesom, an Australian who had achieved the American Dream—money, a mansion, cars, a yacht—as a high-level Hollywood executive. Still, he had thought something was wrong with him because the more he got, the less happy he was. The success that so many people dream of didn't fulfill him.

> *Don't aim at success—the more you aim at it and make it a target, the more you are going to miss it. For success, like happiness, cannot be pursued; it must ensue, and it only does so as the unintended side-effect of one's dedication to a cause greater than oneself.* (Viktor Frankl, *Man's Search for Meaning,* pp. xiv-xv)

In 2003, Scott took a vacation to Cambodia and visited the Stung Meanchey garbage dump outside Phnom Penh, where he saw thousands of desperate children searching for food scraps in a massive, toxic garbage dump the size of several football fields. He spoke to a little girl with the help of a translator and asked her questions about her circumstances. This experience changed him.

Scott returned home, gave up his high salary and Hollywood lifestyle, sold all his fancy stuff, and moved full-time to Cambodia to start helping those kids. He used his own money and donations from friends to create the Cambodian Children's Fund, which works with children, families, and communities to restore health, provide education, and offer effective leadership skills to children. At the time of our visit, Scott's organization had rescued, housed, clothed, fed, and educated 1,954 children.

As our group sat at lunch tables and were served by a large group of the children, we saw a slide show set to the music of Coldplay's song, *Fix You*. On the left side of the screen appeared a photo of the baby or child on the day they were rescued at the dump; on the right was a photo of the child now. Set to the rhythm of the song, we saw before-and-after photos of child after child, their transformation into physical health apparent, the sparkle of light having returned to their eyes.

In 2009, the garbage dump was closed, and now Scott's organization works with destitute families in the area. Its goal is to provide resources for fostering health, dignity, education, and leadership, all of which create a foundation for moving from survival mode to creating a meaningful future.

Six of these older kids talked to our group. What caught my attention was their passion to help their community, their country, and the larger world. They wanted to protect the environment; they wanted to teach; they wanted to help the impoverished; they wanted to work in medicine. Once they had healed enough physically and emotionally, they wanted to contribute to the world around them. As I watched them speak to us, what struck me most of all was even though, like Viktor, they had suffered enormous losses, losses that could easily define a whole life, they were more in love with the future than they were with the past!

Viewed against my own history, this relatively short-term shift in their psychological healing was remarkable. How did they do it so quickly? I've been working my ass off all my life to move forward from painful circumstances, and I'm just now waking up to a deeper sense of meaning, and (as Viktor described) the deep joy that follows! To be more in love with one's future than with one's past clearly marks the end of victimhood. It's a trait of any truly joyful person! What allowed these children to heal so quickly?

The key is something I haven't experienced around my pain: a narrative shared by an entire community. Every Cambodian endured the genocide; every Cambodian family was affected by it, so no Cambodian can possibly be untouched by it. Cambodians share a coherent narrative about what happened and why. Even though each of these orphans and destitute children has a singular story involving their mom, their dad, their siblings, and their grandparents, every singular story exists in the context of a larger, shared story that belongs to the whole country.

These kids aren't orphans or destitute because they are inherently bad, and they are not uniquely broken or alone. The coherent narrative protects them from the isolation of that rabbit hole. Instead, they hurt in the context of their community; each singular story is but one thread in a giant shared tapestry.

A coherent narrative is an essential basis for feeling a sense of belonging. In my case, as I was growing up I didn't know other adopted people, so I thought I was a freak. Even as adults told me I was special and that my adoption was a beautiful thing, I felt the opposite. I experienced something like being a drop of oil in a glass of water; an invisible force field, a permanent barrier, existed between our opposite narratives, so I couldn't reach out to any people in my life or let them come in.

When I was seven, I got a letter from one of my mom's friends, written on yellow stationary with pink bunnies and wisps of green grass.

> *Dear Pam, I was thinking about you tonight, and marveled at how you've been blessed not once, but twice, so early in life. First by a mother who loved you enough to give you up, and second by parents that love you enough to make you their own. Sweet dreams, little one.*

My reaction was, *Huh?*

> *Dear Nice Lady, Really? Did my mom love me enough to give me away? Because my parents gave my first dog away, and that didn't feel like love to me.*

We can say weird things to each other, sometimes to make terrible situations seem more palatable. In those situations, when people fall short of a loving response, grieving people lose a sense of community. And when they finally find a community, perhaps a hospice group or a cancer support group, some of their first bonding is around how terrible it feels when the world says those weird things to them.

This is where, as tragic and brutal as the Cambodian genocide was and still is, a shared and coherent narrative helps the children find their strength and agency more quickly.

For me, the lack of a coherent narrative became an impossible social barrier. *How do I connect with other people if what I feel inside is different from what I'm told I should feel? What do I do if I can't find anything outside of me that feels like it does inside of me? Do I lie and pretend I'm fine when I'm not? Intellectually take being adopted off the table and decide it's no big deal so I can finally leave my own experience and connect with their narrative? Become likable so no one gives me away again?* I tried it all and none of it worked.

To this day the government has my original birth certificate, and I am not legally allowed to see it, but I know what's on it because when I was 25, my adoptive parents and I went to the county courthouse. My parents were the plaintiffs in my adoption case, so they were allowed to see the whole file, but they could see it only if I waited outside the room. My parents saw that my original name was Diana Lynn. Even today when I tell people this story, they are shocked that such laws remain in place. This is just one story, but it's a piece of the wall that still separates me from a sense of belonging in a culture which has a mistaken narrative about adoption.

Years ago, a neighbor of mine lost her husband suddenly and tragically. Even though I was scared to see her anguish, I went to her house to sit with her. I watched her try to eat small bites of a banana and retch. She apologized for retching, and I was shocked at the raw intensity of it, but I realized there was so much I still didn't know about what people experience immediately following a sudden death. So much is kept private when it comes to grief.

When we suffer painful losses, we need community more than ever. The right community must be one in which we make sense. If we don't make sense within a community, then it's not our community—instead, it's more of a stressor than a place to get support and help coming back to life.

My therapist in college was the first person to help me find and speak my truth. Our tiny community of two saved the life of the real person who was buried inside of me and who was suffocating in falseness and separation and addiction. That tiny community of two is a big part of why I became a therapist. I wanted to help others not be silently hiding or half-dead inside, but instead find their truth, speak it, and connect, so that being alive here on earth could ultimately matter and even bring joy!

In my 27 years as a professional, I have formed communities of two for many grieving and dying people who felt isolated in their pain. These tiny communities were where I felt most comfortable.

I know I'm not supposed to say this, but in my own ignorant and childlike way, I have envied large groups with coherent narratives, such as the Cambodians. I've envied the Jews, who despite such a horrific history still have intact traditions and each other. My Jewish friends tell me about the holidays of Rosh Hashanah, a time of celebrating the completion of another year, and Yom Kippur, a time of taking stock of one's life. I wish those holidays belonged to me, but they don't. I've envied addicts who meet at churches and then go out for coffee on work nights. I'm sure I would have been eligible to join them. I've even envied the orphans who grew up in orphanages because at least they could huddle together in the night and say *I don't have parents. I don't have family. I lost everything.* Mainstream culture doesn't so easily put happy frosting on top of their sad story.

I still didn't know how to find a real community for me. I was welcomed by the AIDS Lifecycle community. I love being connected to Camp Kesem. But I (with pleasure) adapt to their agendas and needs. I didn't know if there was a real community out there for me—one that understood my history.

Haley Radke, an adoptee in Canada, started a podcast called *Adoptees On*. She interviewed me a few times—I was the voice of "a therapist who is also adopted." She also interviewed Anne Heffron, who wrote *You Don't Look Adopted*. I listened to Anne's story and liked her immediately. I liked her so much, in fact, that I contacted her to see if she'd give me a coaching session. That was two years ago, and we have been on the phone daily ever since.

We talk about the problem of cultural loneliness as adoptees. Without a coherent narrative, what choice is there for adoptees but to become so frustrated that we deny or kill off vital parts of the self? And then what's left of us? A quiet, grateful mask? I'd never had a friend I could speak with so frankly about issues that had plagued me my whole life, issues that no one outside of me seemed aware of.

Months into our friendship, Anne wrote me a "sister letter" and a contract. If back in the 1960s a contract had legally tied us to adoptive families, why couldn't we make a contract of our own now that we had a choice? We realized with some surprise and joy that we were no less related to each other than we had been to our adoptive families, so why couldn't we be sisters? Here's the beginning of her letter:

> *September 27, 2017*
> *Dear Pam,*
>
> *I have wanted a sister for so long I forgot about the wanting. I got used to so many things so early: these parents are your parents but not your real parents. These brothers are your brothers but not your real brothers. The mirrors you look in will never truly reflect you so please stop looking. The world is not able to reflect you because your mother did not keep you, so it's all about just pretending that things are normal. You can do that, right? You're a good girl.*
>
> *Guess what?*
>
> *It's about me now. I am ready to seek my reflection in the world, and from the moment I first heard your voice on Haley's show, I thought: her. She's mine. I will have your back so heartily I will push you forward. I will sister you.*

From our community of two, Anne and I looked for solutions to the deep sense of isolation of other adult adoptees. We designed a four-day retreat to create bonding and dignity, the bases of any healthy community. *Call and Response. You matter because you're alive. You belong.*

The first night of the retreat, we say, *Raise your hand if you're adopted,* and we all look around the room like we've seen a ghost—not just the participants, but Anne and me, too. It's still so odd to see adults who had been babies who lost it all—to babies, parents are everything—and who survived the loss and landed together in a room, alive and still hoping for something better.

In these retreats, among these kindred spirits, my elevator in the coat closet finally reaches its destination; the doors open, and astonished, I walk into the warmth of a coherent narrative.

Any group can do this with the same effect: *Raise your hand if you've lost someone irreplaceable. Raise your hand if you have metastatic cancer. Raise your hand if you have a mentally ill child. Raise your hand if you've lost a child.* Coherent narrative is the basis for trust and healing.

It's heavy and exhilarating to share a long weekend with kindred spirits. Bubbles of joy begin to erupt once we feel understood and loved. On the third night of our retreats, Anne and I have the group lie on their backs in a circle, heads in the center, and do "Laughing Yoga." We make ourselves laugh until we are truly laughing so hard we can't stop. Crying laughing. The pain that brought us together has evolved into a festive celebration of community, a celebration of the strength we feel collectively and the joy we can risk once we feel deeply understood.

In my private practice, I found myself working with older women, most of them widows, who kept telling me the same stories that they couldn't tell their families, their friends, or their neighbors. *I don't know if I can make it without him. I don't want to be alive without him. I don't feel strong enough. This is the worst nightmare of my life.*

What kept occurring to me is these women needed each other more than they needed me! They needed to draw on the strength of a community in which the depths of their pain made sense, in which they could heal into a meaningful future together. So I created a group of grieving older women, and nine of them have been meeting with me on Thursdays. Together, we navigate the coherent narrative of grief as well as the power of stepping into another giant truth: they are still alive! We explore a question Viktor would ask, *What is life asking of you now?*

A healthy, healing community has one foot grounded in the truth of pain, without distorting it into hopelessness or false positivity, and another foot grounded in Direct Experience, which is where we heal. Three years later, the members of our Thursday group have a firm grasp on the reality of their grief. Their coherent narrative nourishes them like fertile soil. They also recognize the preciousness of the moment at hand, where they can experience new growth like a plant that has been stressed but manages to survive. They find hope for their future, with the possibility that their lives may yet again bloom, despite their profound losses.

When I hold group with these ladies, I often feel like a strict schoolteacher: I must continually remind them to keep the volume of their voices and laughter down because others in the building are having therapy sessions. These women are full of delight in their community.

Some groups only go partway. They, too, meet in their shared pain and have a coherent narrative, but they churn together in a culture of blame and victimhood. These communities are doing their best—they just don't know what actually helps and what doesn't. As with individuals, the Default Network cannot be in charge of a healthy, effective community because it reinforces and rigidifies patterns of pain in its members. The Default Network only knows how to stay hooked into the pain of the past, hooked into coping, blaming, and staying "against."

Having observed the models of the California AIDS Lifecycle community and Camp Kesem, I now understand that a healing community has three essential components.

The first is a shared, coherent narrative.

The second is a search for a collective vision on how to move forward. The California AIDS Ride raises millions of dollars each year to improve the quality of life for people living with HIV/AIDS. Camp Kesem provides free summer camps for grieving children. Anne and I create healing retreats for adoptees. Cynthia and I lead people in transition on a transformative walking journey along the Camino de Santiago.

The third component of community is rare, but essential: the joyful celebration of life itself. This component does not deny or minimize the pain that brought everyone together in the first place, but instead expresses another essential truth: we are alive!

Most mornings on the AIDS Ride I dreaded the sound of my alarm at 4:15 a.m. My body was cooked. I couldn't imagine facing another day on the saddle, peddling up hill after hill. On these mornings I whispered to myself, *I'm never, EVER doing this again!* But Day 5 was different. From my sleeping bag I heard excited whispers and gasps. When I peeked out of my tent, I saw a surprising sea of glamorous red.

It was "Red Dress Day," one of the most festive traditions on the California AIDS Ride. In the beginning it was called "Dress in Red Day" because, by wearing red, the string of cyclists would look like a giant red ribbon working its way through the many switchbacks of the Day 5 route.

No longer do the 3,000 cyclists simply wear red—they must wear red dresses! Prom dresses, flapper dresses, ball gowns, corset dresses, tutu dresses, off-the-shoulder dresses—any dress will do. We accessorize with jewelry, wigs, stockings, even stiletto clip-on bike shoes! Red Dress Day is a party from dawn to dusk, and it's so festive that we forget how deep-down exhausted we are as we peddle on toward our destination.

We are in Red Dresses! We said Yes to the chance to help others! We are alive!

In *The Power of Myth*, Joseph Campbell said,

> *But suddenly you're ripped into being alive. And life is pain, and life is suffering, and life is horror, but my god you're alive and it's spectacular.* (The PBS Series *The Power of Myth* with Bill Moyers, 1988)

A community must go all the way to ***We're alive and it's spectacular*** to reach its potential. A community like this will continually remind you of your greatest potential because the members of that community are reaching theirs. Anything short of spectacular is like living on that miserable fence I had been on for so long: neither fully alive nor fully dead.

But the truth is you're alive—and it's spectacular!

Questions for Reflection:

1. Who are your people? In which classes or jobs or groups have you felt the most at home? Who is your chosen family?
2. Who which people in the world do you share a coherent narrative? Who understands the deepest parts of you? Who accepts things about you that others in the world may not easily accept?
3. If you have a community, how big a role does the Default Network play in your conversations and activities? What would it be like to reduce the Default Network's role? What would your community talk about and do then?
4. When in community have you experienced a joyful celebration of life itself? Was it a family occasion? A neighborhood event? In the wake of a crisis? On a vacation? What did that joyful celebration mean to you, and how does the rest of your life compare to that moment?

Actions to Immediately Increase Your Life Force:

1. Go online and try to find people (strangers) in the world who speak your language and relate to your deepest pain or shame. For example, I found Haley Radke's podcast *Adoptees On* to listen to the stories and feelings of other adoptees. I wrote to her. She responded and now we are friends. This connection led me to Anne and other new friends. Write a note to someone you find. It doesn't matter if they respond to you or not—what matters is you've taken an action to honor your resonance with them. You've stepped into community with a coherent narrative. It's a start.

2. Start to search for (or consider creating) a community that meets a need you have. It could be a community based in grief or sobriety or creativity or fitness or a social justice issue—anything true for you. I have a friend who has begun supporting women in her community who are trying to raise their young children without repeating trauma from their own childhoods. She is passionate about changing generational patterns, and young moms are flocking to her. Take baby steps in, and notice how it feels to begin moving from *Me* to *We.*

Epilogue

I should have been a statistic—if not a suicide or full-blown addict or murderer, then someone who stayed frozen and half-dead on that fence, never choosing a side, just waiting out my days until I could finally lie down and rest.

But Viktor Frankl flipped the question *Why should I stay alive?* on its head when he asked, *What is life asking of you?*

When pain is so overwhelming that the noise of it consumes us and drowns out the world around us, we are stuck in the distortion of despair. We all know this hellish place, and anyone who stays there too long is in grave danger.

Pain consists of:

- Contraction
- Isolation
- Conservation of Energy
- Self-Enhancement (making *my* life better)

We have to find our way, step by step, again and again, from pain to meaning, the truer place. Having the world change for us is not a requirement of meaning; meaning is available to the most destitute of us—orphans and widows, the sick and the grieving. Viktor and other heroes have proven that.

Meaning feels like:

- Expansion
- Connection
- Openness to Growth
- Self-Transcendence (a life beyond *me*)

The 10 Foundations are the bridges between these worlds. May they help you step more deeply into your own life, for yourself and for the world who needs you—the real you—at your brightest.

1. To Bond, you must practice Call and Response.
2. You have Dignity every moment simply because you are alive.
3. You only heal in Direct Experience.
4. Attitude is your power in any moment.
5. Creativity: Find your wholehearted Yes.
6. Suffering: Meaning is the answer to despair.
7. Responsibility and Freedom go hand in hand.
8. Your Future Self is wiser than you are.
9. Banishing Against-ness strengthens our causes.
10. "Spectacular" Community must include the joy of being alive.

Any one of these foundations can significantly improve your life. Working on all 10 will awaken greater meaning, joy, and peace. I've clawed my way to each of them, and I claw my way back to them when I forget. You deserve the power of these foundations, and the world deserves a wholehearted you.

Dear Viktor,

I still have questions for you— not because I struggle with WHY to say Yes to life, but because sometimes I still have questions about HOW.

When did you decide to climb your first post-Holocaust mountain? Were you searching for something in the climb?

What was it like as you stepped your way to the top? Was the summit exhilarating? Fortifying? Bittersweet?

What was it like when you held your daughter for the first time, when you held a brand new life instead of the hand of a dying prisoner?

When despair visited, did you stay with it, allowing suffering to continue? Or did you shift your focus to meaning, to the life right in front of you? How did you navigate these choices?

Thank you for giving my heart the courage to choose life and for teaching me that saying Yes is the only way to live. Wait—did you give my heart courage, or did I? It's confusing. I think we did it together. Some things are too hard to do alone.

With love and the deepest gratitude,
Pam

Acknowledgements

Heartfelt thank you to . . .

My husband Tom for your loving heart and unwavering devotion. I told you in college that I'd be happy to hang out with you anywhere—even at a garbage dump. You are home.

Lauren and Sarah, our daughters. No one has been more directly impacted by my history than you; yet you are brave and spirited enough to blaze trails in your own lives with authenticity and heart. I am in the front row cheering you on!

Anne, for reaching into my soul to fiercely champion the best of me while scoffing mercilessly at the outdated messages of my survival brain. You're a supersonic friend, mentor, and cribmate.

Becki, my sister since 7th grade. You are a constant in my days. Knowing that we understand and love each other no matter what gives me great peace.

Cynthia, my companion in navigating everything "Meaning." Our learning adventures and wild conversations have catapulted my understanding of invisible forces that shape us—meaning, consciousness, and love.

Claude, for helping me heal things in my brain that I thought were beyond repair and for saving the integrity of my family.

Jamie, for consistently bringing enthusiasm, clarity, and vision to our work together. And for always seeing the best in me, even when I couldn't.

Alan, editor extraordinaire, for your wise and generous care with this book. You helped me during a very busy time in your life, and I am grateful because I couldn't have navigated this manuscript without you.

Clients, group members, and retreat participants who have taught me firsthand about our innate human capacity for resilience and who generously allowed me to share their stories in this book.

Camp Kesem counselors who inspire my life with youthful energy and make me want to be a better person.

About the Author

Pam Cordano, MFT is a psychotherapist, cancer survivor, and adoptee who is passionate about healing in community. Most of her work over 27 years has been focused on clients who experience serious illness or tragedy, where life was one way and suddenly changed on a dime. Her early life experience mirrors the trauma of this population, and her personal insights have deeply influenced her work.

Pam's greatest passion is helping people awaken their human capacity to move from despair to finding a deeper Yes to life. Inspired by Viktor Frankl, she helps clients identify and cultivate what is uniquely meaningful to them, which allows for increased vitality and new possibilities.

Pam is particularly interested in the power of community to catalyze healing and growth. She leads weekly Meaning Groups in her private practice and facilitates local and international healing retreats. Recently, Pam has begun integrating community and travel by bringing groups of adults on transformational journeys to the Camino de Santiago in Spain. www.pamcordano.com

Printed in the United States
By Bookmasters